Will Write for Shoes

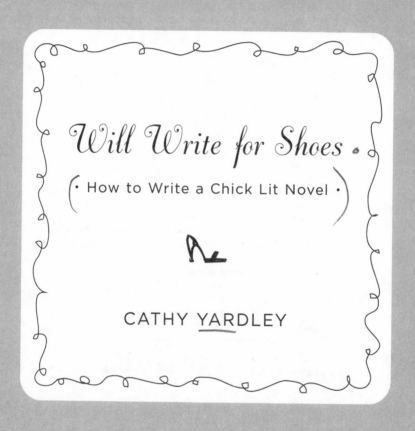

Will Write for Shoes

(• How to Write a Chick Lit Novel •)

CATHY YARDLEY

THOMAS DUNNE BOOKS
St. Martin's Press
New York

THOMAS DUNNE BOOKS.
An imprint of St. Martin's Press.

www.thomasdunnebooks.com
www.stmartins.com

BOOK DESIGN BY AMANDA DEWEY

Library of Congress Cataloging-in-Publication Data

Yardley, Cathy.
Will write for shoes : how to write a chick lit novel / Cathy Yardley.—1st ed.
p. cm.

Includes index.

ISBN-13: 978-0-312-35899-0
ISBN-10: 0-312-35899-7
1. Chick lit—Authorship. I. Title

PN3377.5.C45 Y37 2006
808.3085—dc22
2006045053

First Edition: September 2006

10 9 8 7 6 5 4 3 2 1

To the Deadline Hellions

CONTENTS

I. It's a Chick's World

II. Where Do I Sign Up?
How to Write a Chick Lit Novel

III. *Baby Needs a New Pair of Shoes . . .*
The Crapshoot That Is Selling Your Novel

IV. Frequently Asked Questions

APPENDIXES
(Mostly) Useful Information

.I.

*It's a
Chick's World*

1.

What Is Chick Lit?

I started writing in 1995, after I had graduated from Berkeley and moved to Los Angeles to find work and to stay with my college boyfriend. I planned on writing romance novels, because they had helped me keep my sanity while I pursued a double major. After a few years in Los Angeles, and after I'd sold my first romance novel, I realized that I had a story idea that didn't fit in the relatively rigid parameters of romance. It was a story about three women trying to figure out how they were supposed to live life, with Los Angeles as a background. I had no idea who would buy it or where it would fit in, so I tucked it away on the shelf. Then, in 2000, rumors began to emerge about a new kind of women's fiction—one they were tentatively calling "city girl books." In fact, that was the original name of the Chick Lit line that Harlequin produced. Bridget Jones burst onto the scene; articles were being written up. I had found the perfect niche for my quirky, humorous, coming-of-age stories.

When I tell people outside of the writing community that I write Chick Lit, they usually wear a polite, humoring smile. Those that are avid readers usually give me a patronizing smirk—*oh, you write* those *books.* The thing is, if I asked any one of them to define Chick Lit, they would not have a clear answer. They'd probably say, "Those are those dating books, right? The ones with the bright pink covers?" Or they would shrug and say that, although they don't know how to define it, they know it when they see it. Like art. Or, you know, pornography.

I'm here to tell you Chick Lit isn't what they think it is. It probably isn't even what you think it is. And the parameters and definitions for Chick Lit are evolving daily.

Although by no means the be-all, end-all definition, this is my own description of the Chick Lit genre: Chick Lit is a subgenre of the larger classification of women's fiction, generally a coming-of-age or "coming-of-consciousness" story where a woman's life is transformed by the events of the story. Again, I'm sure you'll be able to see exceptions to the rule (that darned Shopaholic girl is barely transformed if credit woes continue to be her conflict in book after book) but for the most part, you see a woman or women change for the better in a Chick Lit novel. They're usually fairly upbeat, too. You're not going to see "uplifting" stories in the Oprah-book-club definition of the term (which is generally a way of saying, "You'll be weeping like the first time you saw *Titanic*"). Chick Lit generally has a sense of humor. It has a funny tone and voice, but, more important, the characters don't take themselves too seriously, no matter how dire the circumstances. My favorite examples of this are Marian Keyes's books. Infidelity, pregnancy, Hodgkin's disease, drug addiction . . . she tackles all these topics, but still manages to be funny about them, in startlingly effective ways. As a general rule, Chick Lit deals with topics that affect a woman's life. So: friendship dynamics. Glass ceilings. Over-nurturing. Kids and biological clocks. And, of course, love.

Is this to say that women have absolutely no interest in things like, say, global warming, gas prices, genetic engineering, or even the shotgun formation? Of course not. Is Chick Lit meant to "write down" to women by appealing to these subjects? *Absolutely not.* Still, these topics are truly important to women, and rubbing it in their faces that "wanting a husband when there's a hole in the ozone layer is frivolous" is not only intellectual snobbery, it's pointless. And if you don't believe that, then you could very well be an excellent writer, but you're not going to be writing Chick Lit. Good luck with another aisle in the bookstore.

For those writers who take offense at reviewers and critics who call Chick Lit "fluffy," "frothy," or "dumb" and who want to counter by making Chick Lit novels literary heavyweights, I have only one piece of advice: *switch to decaf.* Seriously. As Chick Lit authors, we'll have messages, themes, and insights, of course. But our primary job is to entertain. We're not finding the cure to cancer here.

At the same time, the best compliment I ever got was from a reader at a book signing in Los Angeles. Her mother had died, she told me. During that apparently lengthy process, when she was frantic with stress and melancholy, she reread my first Chick Lit book, *L.A. Woman,* over and over. It comforted her and gave her a mental escape.

If you can do that, entertain and comfort, and maybe even give some insight, then you've done your job.

2.

A Brief History of Chick Lit

In the beginning, there was Bridget.

That's not entirely true—there were Chick Lit books in circulation in England for some time before anyone realized a trend was starting—but by all accounts, the Chick Lit wave started with a British invasion, spearheaded by one plucky young "singleton" by the name of Bridget Jones. The fictional creation of Helen Fielding, the book took America by storm. With wit and a certain irrepressible spirit, the book managed to capture the attention of thirtysomething women who felt like they, too, had a shelf life—women in dead-end jobs whose greatest fears included dying alone and being discovered half-eaten by dogs. It took very real concerns and put a hilarious spin on them.

If nothing else, it told America what the heck "snogging" meant.

Before Helen Fielding made snogging accessible, there was another writer creating waves on the other side of the pond. Irish author Marian Keyes, considered the godmother of Chick Lit, was creating her now famous Walsh sister series. It opens with *Watermelon*, the story of Claire Walsh, and starts with her husband leaving her the day she has their first child. While the story premise seems traumatic (and indeed, it *is* traumatic for Claire), it is the archetypical Chick Lit story: woman's life disintegrates, woman's life changes radically after many mishaps, woman comes out a stronger, happier person in the end. All told with what could be characterized as the "Chick Lit" tone.

Whereas previous women's fiction, by authors such as Maeve Binchy, usually had a high angst factor and a tone of stoic resolve, these new Chick Lit books had a fair dose of humor. Irreverent in tone, these novels were characterized by sharp internal observations, a fair dose of comedic venting, and sharp-as-a-razor dialogue. In the case of Bridget Jones, it also involved an unashamed pursuit of slapstick humor. The key factor that set it apart: the stories and main characters did not take themselves, or their tragedies, too seriously—even if, as in the case of Marian Keyes's novels, the underlying premise dealt with substantial issues ranging from infidelity to drug addiction.

Chick Lit might have been a purely British import if it weren't for the next book, Melissa Bank's *The Girls' Guide to Hunting and Fishing*. Rather than a novel, it was an anthology of short stories, all linked in one way or another. Were it not for the breakout success of Helen Fielding and several other British authors, it might have been swallowed whole and gone unnoticed by the literary fiction world. However, *Girls' Guide* was soon crowned the first American Chick Lit book. Many others soon followed. Shortly after, Jennifer Weiner broke in with *Good in Bed*, and authors such as Jane Green, Anna

Maxted, and others were filling the shelves of the fiction aisles. The next American offering adopted by Chick Lit: *Sex and the City*, by Candace Bushnell. Developed into a television series by HBO, it became a smash hit by projecting what reading audiences already loved about Chick Lit: pop culture, high fashion, urban settings, and women they could relate to. Protagonists were single; in their twenties and thirties; and dealing with shoddy relationships, career troubles, financial issues, and biological clocks, all while maintaining a circle of friends that were, for all intents and purposes, closer than any blood family.

Newsweek and other major publications picked up on the trend: the rise of the single woman. They were recognizing the same factors that made Chick Lit a growing sensation: more women were remaining single longer. These single women had higher incomes and, consequently, more buying power—and they were making that power known in the commercial world. Record numbers of single women were buying houses on their own. Beyond that, according to census numbers, more people were forming "nontraditional households"—not married couples or domestic partnerships, but groups of friends living together, even up to their thirties. This sort of mentality was reflected in the hugely popular sitcom *Friends*, and the friends-as-family-unit model was glorified in the culturally iconic TV show *Seinfeld*. It was a time when car commercials started being targeted at women, when diamond companies started advertising the "right-hand ring" (suggesting that women shouldn't wait for Mr. Right in order to get a rock of their own), and when American publishing companies decided to cash in on the Chick Lit tidal wave.

One of the first publishing companies to capitalize on the trend was Red Dress Ink, an imprint of the huge romance conglomerate

Harlequin. Several American publishers were already bringing in British offsets, but Red Dress Ink was determined to launch and heavily promote American and British novelists using the distribution machine they had perfected with romance novels. Starting with *See Jane Date* by Melissa Senate, they soon brought out one book a month starting in 2002. Their new imprint grew exponentially in the first two years. Quickly thereafter, Simon and Schuster came out with the imprint Downtown Press, a slightly more literary set of offerings, starting with *Getting Over Jack Wagner* by Elise Juska and the innovative novel *The Song Reader* by Lisa Tucker. Avon Trade, Kensington's Strapless imprint, and many others followed. (More details on each publishing house are covered in Chapter 18.)

Chick Lit has grown in leaps and bounds. Many say that the trend is simply a fad, something that has peaked and will soon die out. Of course, they've been saying that for years now. While retail sales for the genre have plateaued, the exponential boom of sales numbers was bound to self-correct once publishers jumped on the bandwagon and saturated the market. The bottom line, however, is that Chick Lit is leveling off. It isn't decreasing. It's not a fad that's going away—it's a mainstream genre that's made an impression and doesn't appear to be fading any time soon.

The fact is, the situations that Chick Lit reported on have not disappeared. The tone and humor that characterize Chick Lit are now popular in not only literature, but television and film projects for both genders. The genre is still evolving and influencing the mainstream. Chick Lit is simply an overgeneralized moniker for contemporary women's fiction, with as many facets and faces as contemporary women themselves have.

It's a great time to write a Chick Lit novel.

3.

Chick Lit 101

The Basics of "Traditional" Chick Lit

Thanks to the "history" of Chick Lit that I've just described to you, there is now a set of characteristics that comprise what could be called "traditional" Chick Lit. They're important elements of early work. In fact, they've been used to the point that many of them are considered Chick Lit clichés. I'll address how to avoid the cliché trap at the end of the chapter. In the meantime, the elements are:

Urban location. If you read early Chick Lit, you'll notice it's almost always set in one of two places: London or New York. (Marian Keyes's Ireland books are the obvious exceptions.) The protagonists are usually young women, often naïve or from smaller towns. The idea behind using an urban location is to provide what is assumed to be a more exciting, fast-paced, high-toned lifestyle. In the television series *Sex and the City*, New York was as much a character as Carrie, Charlotte, Samantha, or Miranda. In my own novel *L.A. Woman*, I deliberately chose Los Angeles for its attention-deficit-disorder sense of entertainment and shallow but glamorous atmosphere. (Keep in mind: I actually *like* Los Angeles!) With a metropolitan setting, you are able to show more expensive clothing, more ethnic diversity, more upscale industries, and more fast-paced lifestyles. The quirks of these locales also serve as plot devices: the impossibility of getting an apartment in New York, say, or the difficulties of living in such a tiny place when you do find something. Of course, it's got to be an *upscale* urban environment. Manhattan, yes . . . but a really rough neighborhood in the Bronx? No, as a general rule.

Glam industries. The women in these exciting cities were usually peons in very glamorous companies. Early on, publishing was a favorite, then fashion houses and advertising agencies. Like the location, these jobs were meant to be fast-paced and high-energy . . . the sort of positions that readers would love to experience vicariously. Seeing models catfight, learning the backstabbing and the war-planning in a big creative company. And the main character was our Cinderella, just watching people get ready for the ball while waiting for her chance to dance. It's the best of both worlds: an exciting, unusual locale, with an underdog protagonist that the reader can identify with as her guide. You see this especially in stories such as *The Devil Wears Prada* by Lauren Weisberger, which goes behind the scenes at a fashion magazine, or *Mim Warner's Lost Her Cool* by Lynn Messina, which covers the trend-spotting efforts of a "cool hunter."

The simply marvelous gay friend. After living in San Francisco and Los Angeles, I can say I've known plenty of gay guys in my day. Early Chick Lit heroines almost always have a gay best friend, someone who can go shoe shopping with them and commiserate on the sorry state of men in whatever city they're in. These best friends are, to a man, fabulous. By that, I mean they are flamboyantly gay, over-the-top gay, "Men on Film" from *In Living Color* gay. Often, they're literal drag queens. They are great characters, but through massive overuse as sidekicks and confidantes, they've become somewhat stock characters. One example out of many: the drag queen in Erica Orloff's *Diary of a Blues Goddess.*

The evil boss. These are the guys (or gals) you love to hate, and they give you plenty of reasons to. If the book's protagonist is our Cinderella, then her boss is the stepmother in all her sinister glory. He/she is sometimes stupid, sometimes smart, sometimes dumb-but-not-that-dumb (as in, dumb enough to be incompetent at his/her job, but smart enough to blame you for it). The evil boss is always malicious, however. On the plus side, the evil boss always gets his/her comeuppance in the end, and it's immensely satisfying. A prime example: Lynn Messina's *Fashionistas.*

The cheating lover. If you see a boyfriend for the Chick Lit heroine somewhere in the first fifty pages of a book and you get a hinky feeling about him—he's good-looking, he's charming, but there's something not quite right—then you've got good instincts. He's cheating on her. Of course, in early Chick Lit, this deception is discovered early on. Usually it's even the inciting incident: the heroine has a terrible day with Evil Boss, then comes home early to find her boyfriend in bed with her best friend/sister/mother/mailman. The cheating lover then may or may not spend a significant portion of the rest of the book trying to win her back. He will almost definitely pop up near the end of the book, saying he's sorry and that he'll make it up to her. This usually screws up whatever decent relationship the heroine is starting. (We know that he doesn't really mean it and usually scream, "Don't do it! Don't go back to him!" as we turn the pages, much like a horror movie where we can't believe the heroine would even consider wandering downstairs into the darkened basement unarmed and alone. And in her underwear, natch.) You can see this example in almost every early Chick Lit novel, starting with Bridget Jones and going right through *Watermelon*.

Drinks, dates, and Mr. Wrongs. For every cheating lover, there is usually a period of time when the protagonist tries to correct the situation by diving into the dating pool. (Drinks-and-dating is another traditional Chick Lit element.) Our protagonist, usually flanked by several of her girlfriends, goes on a man-hunting expedition to a bar, speed-dating event, Internet dating site, what have you. During the course of these adventures, she runs into one "Mr. Wrong" after another. The man who calls his mother long-distance during the dinner date. The man who has anger-management issues and insists that the protagonist pay for everything. The man who has the bad toupee . . . you get the picture. These guys are also stock characters (and a large part of the humor) in early traditional Chick Lit. The first Red Dress Ink novel, *See Jane Date* by Melissa Senate, is a perfect example of this phenomenon.

Life implosion syndrome. It sucks to be a Chick Lit heroine. Why? Because when something goes wrong in a Chick Lit heroine's life, it's not just one thing—it's *everything*. Usually in the first seventy-five pages or so, she winds up losing her job, losing her apartment, finding out the in flagrante delicto truth about her boyfriend, and generally having every single thing she counted on vanish into thin air. The difference between the first quarter of a Chick Lit book and an old disaster flick is the stylish clothes. Perfect example: *Going Coastal* by Wendy French. The purpose of life implosion syndrome is usually to give the heroine a goal to strive toward, namely the repair of her life. Since the heroine is often directionless although plucky, this is the impetus she needs to do something dramatic (which the book then uses as a plot structure). It also takes away all vestiges of security, so the heroine can change during the course of the book, developing her own self-confidence.

"Chick Lit fabulous." Speaking of clothes—maybe it's the cities they live in or the industries they work in, but does anybody else wonder how secretaries, assistants, and other low-level corporate minions like our heroines can afford nice apartments and seem to have wardrobes like Eva Perón? There's a ton of deliberate name-dropping: Prada, Manolo Blahnik, BCBG, Givenchy, Juicy Couture. Why? Again, it's shorthand. It plays directly on a reader's sense of lifestyle envy. Is it realistic? No, probably not. (Although the credit debt these poor heroines are carting around undoubtedly is realistic.) But again, it's for readers who have *It's Good to Be . . .* or *Fabulous Life of* TiVo'd as a guilty pleasure. If not poor protagonists trying to melt their credit cards, then it's rich heiresses or wealthy wives trying to spend their way out of misery. The name-dropping and expensive trappings also puts a sort of sheen of otherworldliness on the whole novel. Prime examples of this: Plum Sykes's *Bergdorf Blondes* and any book from the Shopaholic series.

Club coffee klatch. You especially see this in early Chick Lit. If you watched *Sex and the City*, these would be the scenes where the girls met for brunch or lunch and basically did a dialogue download of whatever was happening in the episode—color commentary, if you will. These wound up being a bulk of the scenes in traditional Chick Lit. (My editor once called it being "trapped in the coffeehouse.") It presents a great chance to show some truly funny witty banter, even if it doesn't really advance the plot a whole lot. There are more examples of this than can be named, but here's one that leaps to mind. Liz Maverick's *What a Girl Wants* has "girly brunches" that showcase some really funny dialogue (the "porn epiphany" still being my favorite) and that actually serve as something of a plot device.

Pop culture, anyone? With traditional Chick Lit, you saw not only a lot of brand name–dropping, but also a lot of references to pop culture occurrences—often without any accompanying explanation. It was as if Chick Lit was an inside joke, and if you weren't twenty or thirty years old (or watched a lot of TV and owned a subscription to *Entertainment Weekly*) then you weren't going to get it. "He thinks he's so Dane Cook," a protagonist might say, never clarifying that Dane Cook is a relatively underground comedian, made popular through MySpace.com and the Cartoon Network. Or people will be text messaging each other in code: TTYL,

BRB, LOL. It's assumed that the audience for Chick Lit *is* in on the joke. And even if they aren't, they'll take the surrounding paragraphs and piece together what the author is saying through context . . . and probably wind up using the same reference in a conversation with their friends later that day.

What's wrong with these elements? Honestly—absolutely nothing. There's a reason they worked for so long. They're identifiable, they're attractive, they serve a purpose. The problem is, they've also been done to death. It's good to write more traditional Chick Lit because there's a market for it; people know what it is and they know what to expect. They're also easily bored. If you're going to use these elements, then you have to use them deliberately, with some purpose in mind. You also should try giving each element a twist. For example, the cheating lover could be framed—or the evil boss made somehow sympathetic, say. I'll get into this more in Chapter 6 on characterization. The point is, the trail has been blazed . . . it's up to you to decide how far to depart from it.

4.

Brave New Chicks

New Trends in Chick Lit

We've just covered the basic elements of "traditional" Chick Lit: the clichés, the stock characters, the basic plot elements. None of these are bad things, although Chick Lit authors have not been satisfied with writing rote plot lines and characters. Moving beyond the bad-dates-and-drinking love stories, Chick Lit has evolved into new and complex subgenres and cross-genres. Here are some examples, although the list is by no means exhaustive. There's plenty of room for change while still retaining the Chick Lit voice and humor.

Chick Lit Mystery and Tart Noir. This subgenre was allegedly started by a group of women mystery writers who dubbed their subversive work "Tart Noir." (You can see the full story on these women on their Web site, www.tartcity

.com.) These stories had women protagonists as hardboiled detectives in the classic vein; some also featured protagonists as murderers, narrated in the first-person point of view. There is often a sense of black humor in these stories. British novels especially embraced this concept: the heroine Samantha Jones from *Black Rubber Dress* by Lauren Henderson is a more-than-casual drug user and avid sexaholic who also happens to be an amateur sleuth. Not to be outdone, more traditional Chick Lit authors got the idea to cross the genres with a gentler blend of sassy storylines and murder solving. The birth of these stories actually predates Tart Noir in the form of one author: Janet Evanovich, author of a mystery series involving one of the world's most unlikely bounty hunters, Stephanie Plum. Evanovich's humorous voice and over-the-top antics, colorful side characters, and rotating love triangle have earned her a rabidly loyal fan base. Other authors followed with their own series: Sarah Strohmeyer with her Bubbles Unbound mysteries, Susan McBride and her Debutante Dropout mystery series . . . the examples are endless, although there's still room to grow in this cross-genre, which is more mainstream-friendly than the Tarts' subversive offerings.

Rise of the Antiheroine. Again, this sort of starts with the Tarts, but is by no means the only example of it. If you write in a commercial genre such as Westerns, sci-fi, mystery, or (especially) romance, as a general rule you want to create heroines who are sympathetic: the reader must like, or at least understand, the female characters you've developed. You'll hear about tons of romance novels that have been rejected because of "unsympathetic characters." A new trend has begun, however, in Hollywood . . . the rise of the antihero, the unsympathetic yet compelling character that stands out against the cookie-cutter ideals of the previous genre standards. Take, for example, Clint Eastwood's performance in *Unforgiven,* or Guy Pearce's brilliant portrayal of Ed Exley in *L.A. Confidential.* You could have an antihero who was still tough, still utterly masculine . . . if anything, his bucking of authority tended to emphasize that, his bad or "unsympathetic" qualities, only making the character more fascinating. Women characters have not usually received this kind of leeway. That is, until now.

In books like Caren Lissner's brilliant novel *Carrie Pilby,* you've got a girl who, on the surface, is the opposite of plucky. She's pessimistic, she's antisocial, and she's not your average girl next door. Instead, she's a nineteen-year-old genius, already graduated from college, who hates leaving her house and who generally fears life. She's not apologetic about any of those facts, either; she doesn't beg the reader's understanding, and there are no tearful and emotionally manipulative scenes where she cares for orphans or feeds puppies or somehow otherwise shows the reader that "really, she's a good girl." Yet her story of overcoming her fears and joining the world touches on elemental truths that make her imminently readable. Then, you've got books like *Fashionistas* by Lynn Messina, or *Are You in the Mood?* by Stephanie Lehmann, which have protagonists who actually do "bad" things—lying, conniving, participating in office warfare, cheating on their significant others (or coming perilously close to it). These acts, which would be considered almost villainous in any other genre, are portrayed in a comedic manner, and you're in on the joke as a reader. You may not be rooting for the protagonist to succeed (and, indeed, she usually gets a humbling comeuppance at some point), but you are compelled to keep turning the pages, and that's the important part.

Small Towns, Chick Lit Style. In traditional Chick Lit, by and large the stories take place in glamorous cosmopolitan settings. After all, how can someone be fabulous in a place like Green Acres? More recently, however, Chick Lit authors have shown that a fabulous attitude and the Chick Lit brand of humor can not only survive but thrive in a rural setting. For some, it's the fish-out-of-water dichotomy: watching someone from a big town flounder ridiculously in a backwater town. (An unfortunate mainstream example of this is Paris Hilton in *The Simple Life*.) Or simply the downshifting of gears: *Rachel's Holiday*, by Marian Keyes, shows the protagonist going from New York City back to her hometown in Ireland, to a small rehab center called the Cloisters. The slower atmosphere only accentuates how crazed her previous life was and allows both Rachel and the reader to examine Rachel's life as if under a microscope, from a completely different perspective. On the other side of the coin, the less cosmopolitan heroine is also getting her day in the sun. Case in point: *Mean Season* by Heather Cochran. Touching, funny, and yet also painfully poignant, this story has a small-town fan club president coming to the disconcerting realization that her hunky Hollywood hero has more than feet of clay. The small hometown plays a significant part in the development of the story.

Mommy Lit. Early Chick Lit usually had protagonists in

their twenties and thirties, living a single life. Their conflicts and woes typically stemmed from unfulfilling love lives or career issues. As Chick Lit heroines grew up, a new subgenre emerged, dealing specifically with the problems that women with children deal with, still using the familiar humor and tongue-in-cheek voice, and often mixed with still traditional elements of Chick Lit: being a Mommy who's trying to "keep up with the Joneses" in New York, as in *Play Dates* by Leslie Carroll. Or being a mother as well as a wife and a career woman, with the challenge of trying to balance all these elements. The ultimate example of this is Allison Pearson's *I Don't Know How She Does It*. Similar to small-town settings, there is typically a fish-out-of-water element to it— often with new mothers who are completely ill-prepared to go from a life of clubbing-carousing-whatever to the realities of full-time motherhood.

Lady Lit or Hen Lit. Does a woman lose her Chickness when she gets to a certain age? The answer: absolutely not. Chick Lit is an attitude, and as the late Aaliyah sang, age ain't nothin' but a number. So the genre is morphing to encompass the still spirited yet chronologically older protagonist. The novels tackle issues such as older children moving home, late pregnancy, or menopause, as well as age-appropriate takes on the usual themes such as dating (usually after divorce, in this case) or finding one's life purpose. The best author example of this: Jeanne Ray. Her book *Julie and Romeo* has protagonists who are in their sixties, as does her novel *Step-Ball-Change*. Books like *The First Wives Club* by Olivia Goldsmith could easily fit in the Chick Lit definition. And, with the breakout success of television shows like *Desperate House-*

wives, be prepared for a whole slew of novels with forty-plus-aged protagonists. It's an idea whose time has more than come.

Widow Lit. This is a much more specialized area, and a tricky proposition at that, but there are enough novels dealing with this topic to consider it a bona fide subgenre of Chick Lit. One of the best examples of this is *Good Grief* by Lolly Winston. Showing how a woman copes with her husband's death (including going into work in her pajamas and bunny slippers, as illustrated on the cover) gives a very serious subject a humorous, and yet still emotionally charged, treatment. These books do not trivialize the gravity of the situation, but rather show the universality of loss and what I would call a prime and necessary element of Chick Lit novels, the ultimate resilience of the protagonist. This inner strength is often prefaced with completely relatable, completely understandable, and sometimes hilarious missteps.

Bride Lit. This is a very specialized niche, focusing on weddings and the insanity that seems to surround them. Everything from the expenses, the stress of commitment (and any cold-feet issues), and, of course, the nightmare of one's own family and the new in-laws. *Diary of a Mad Bride* by Laura Wolf is a sterling example of this.

Full-Figured Chick Lit. This is also a specialized niche, but it's one that has been present since early traditional Chick Lit, with Jennifer Weiner's book *Good in Bed*. This novel introduced a heroine who is forced to deal with her full-figured status when her ex-boyfriend writes about it in a national column. Her subsequent weight loss and psychological life change is the crux of the novel. There are now many novels that tackle body-image issues and weight issues. Some examples are *Fat Chance* by Deborah Blumenthal and *The Weight-Loss Diaries* by Courtney Rubin.

Young Adult Chick Lit. These books are generally called Young Adult or YA, but browse any teen section in the bookstore and you'll be able to spot this cross-genre from twenty paces. Wrapped in candy-colored covers and splashed with cute illustrations, the humorous voice is what pegs these Chick Lit novels. Like Hen Lit, these "junior versions" prove that age is irrelevant. Granted, there are some vocabulary differences, but don't think that these shorter novels are somehow "dumbed down" versions of the real thing. Savvy, smart, and often turbulently emotional, stories like *Big Mouth and Ugly Girl* by Joyce Carol Oates are brilliant stories for any age group. Then there are the fun offerings, like *Knocked Out by My Nunga-Nungas* by Louise Rennison, which is basically Bridget Jones for the under-fifteen crowd. Several popular Chick Lit authors are jumping on the YA bandwagon. And there are even YA antiheroines and "fabulous" lifestyle elements. For shock value, try reading the Gossip Girl series by Cecily von Ziegesar. The frank depictions of sex and drug use in a high-toned high school in New York show that YA is not necessarily for the faint of heart looking to write a fun-and-fluffy youth piece. (If you get freaked out by that, incidentally, a dose of Meg Cabot's Princess series can be something of a balm.) Just keep in mind your target: YA's are not read by teens, but by "tweens" . . . the nine-to-eleven crowd. Odds are good that if they're in their teens, they're reading your adult Chick Lit novels. Also, no matter what age they are, they are savvy enough to find you in the adult section if they liked your book in YA. Unless you want eleven-year-olds reading your adult Chick Lit, you might take a cue from other Chick Lit authors, such as Katie MacAlister and Marianne Mancusi, and write your YA titles under a different pseudonym.

Lad Lit. Jokingly called "Dick Lit," this is the humor and angst of Chick Lit, told from a male point of view. Like Chick Lit, this genre also started "on the other side of the pond," in England. The father of this particular subgenre? Nick Hornby, author of *High Fidelity* and *About a Boy*. (You may have seen the film adaptations of either or both.) The authors are usually male as well, not surprisingly, and the issues this genre tackles relate to the masculine point of view on dating, jobs, and life direction. Lad Lit is a very specialized form, and other than Nick, it hasn't really captured the reading market the way Chick Lit has.

Paranormal Chick Lit. Sci-fi, fantasy, anything with magic . . . only with Chick Lit flair. The boom in this market can almost certainly be attributed to Joss Whedon's brilliant TV series *Buffy the Vampire Slayer*, whose witty banter and kick-ass heroine dealt with all the usual Chick Lit issues: career problems, purpose in life, romantic dramas, family disasters. The vampire subgenre especially got a shot in the arm with MaryJanice Davidson's brilliant *Undead and Unwed*, now a series revolving around the protagonist Betsy Taylor, fashion shoe fetishist and unwitting queen of the vampires. Even time travel got into the act, with Marianne Mancusi's *A Connecticut Fashionista in King Arthur's Court*. There is plenty of room in this cross-genre for more innovation, and with the rise of the supernatural in Hollywood, the sky's the limit.

Ethnic Chick Lit. These subgenres are flourishing. African American Chick Lit is selling well, with books like *Bling* by Erica Kennedy. Hispanic Chick Lit is huge, thanks to *The Dirty Girls Social Club* by Alisa Valdes-Rodriguez and its sequels. Asian Chick Lit has carved its niche with books like *The Dim Sum of All Things* by Kim Wong Keltner. And even Eastern Indian Chick Lit is weighing in, with books like *The Hindi-Bindi Club* and *Goddess for Hire.* While showing the universality of Chick Lit issues and elements, these novels also give mainstream readers a taste of a culture completely different from their own, appealing to women across the ethnic spectrum.

Christian Chick Lit. This is a booming market right now. It has all the attitude and elements of traditional Chick Lit, with one notable difference: the main character is Christian, and the books espouse an attitude and mind-set that reflect that ideology. While they should not, ideally, be "preachy" (depending on the publisher you go with), they usually have no swearing and no premarital sex. Some examples: Kristin Billerbeck's *She's All That* or *Mom Over Miami* by Annie Jones.

Chick Lit Nonfiction. If it can be marketed to women with Chick Lit trappings, it *will* be marketed to women with Chick Lit trappings. Case in point: the pink-and-sage-green cover of *He's Just Not That Into You* by Greg Behrendt and Liz Tuccillo, or the bright magenta hardcover of *Cooking for Mr. Latte,* which is both memoir and cookbook combined, as well as the documentation of a true love story between a *New York Times* food writer and a writer for *The New Yorker.* There are also a slew of how-to books aimed at the Chick Lit reader: The Bad Girl's Guide series, *Stitch 'n Bitch* (a Chick Lit–flavored knitting guide) as well as a host of financial planning, repair, and self-help books. (My favorite so far: a book on witchcraft with a Chick Lit–style illustration on the cover, called *The Joy of Hex*.) The fact that the marketing and voice of Chick Lit has spilled over from the fiction aisles is the ultimate proof that Chick Lit is not a series of stock elements, but an attitude.

There are more cross-genres to be hatched incorporating this attitude. The trick is finding one you are eminently suited to write, and then writing it.

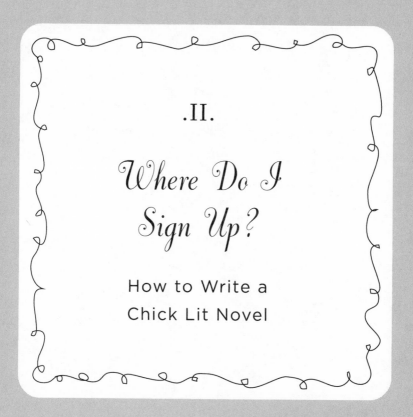

.II.

Where Do I Sign Up?

How to Write a Chick Lit Novel

5.

What's It All About?

Premise

I f you've decided to write a Chick Lit novel, then odds are good you've got some sort of premise. That's the underlying idea for your book. You may hear the term "high-concept premise" bandied about if you hang out with writers who are a bit further along on the writing food chain, or if you listen to editors, who will probably say that's what they're looking for. Rest assured: I've yet to hear someone define what "high-concept" means with any kind of clarity and certainly not with any kind of succinctness. So here's my stab at it (and trust me, it's not clear or succinct, either!):

> **High-concept:** *adjective.* A story idea that can be summed up in one sentence (maximum twenty-five words) that has an intriguing commercial hook.

That's vastly oversimplifying, but here are some high-concept premise examples that might better illustrate what it means.

- *Undead and Unwed* by MaryJanice Davidson: A ditzy fashionista becomes queen of the vampires with hilarious results.
- *The Thin Pink Line* by Lauren Baratz-Logsted: A woman who fakes pregnancy to gain family approval discovers disaster looming as the nine-month mark approaches.
- *Me vs. Me* by Sarah Mlynowski: A strange turn of events allows a woman to live two versions of her life simultaneously—pursuing her career in one life, and then when she falls asleep, switching to the life where she focuses on her marriage.

You might read these sentences and think, "Well, that's just a summary. What's so high-concept about that?" And, in part, you'd be right. The trick is to find the right words to summarize. Something in that sentence needs to be jarring enough to make the reader (in this case, an agent or editor) sit up and take notice. In the first case, for *Undead and Unwed*, it's the contradiction: "ditzy fashionista" and "vampire." (Side note: be careful of using the tag "with hilarious results" or anything similar. It's a shortcut, and it's a dangerous one, since you're basically trying to get the reader to do the heavy lifting for you. The premise has to have the germs of a funny concept to begin with, or you'll look crazy. For example: "Couple gets stranded on island with no food, only knives and hunger . . . and hilarity ensues.")

In the second and third examples, it's the scenarios themselves—setups with just enough ingenuity or unusual twists to make the reader ask, "How does that work?" They're interesting—and they're different enough to stand out. It's not just a rehashing of what's been seen for years, as in, "A woman loses her job, boyfriend, and apartment, only to move back home. The unique angle: it's set in Pittsburgh." If you're going to stand out, you're going to have to do so in a large way, not just differentiating yourself in the details. If you don't have a big enough hook, they'll never get to the details.

But before we get into that, there's a more important question: do you really have a story, or do you just have a cool idea?

This seems like a dumb question, but it's really not. You'd be amazed at how many people have "a cool idea for a book," but on further examination, you find out that they've just got an interesting character, or a neat plot twist . . . and nothing else. No structure, no conflict, nada. That's not a story, that's a cocktail party conversation with other writers.

STORY TESTING FOR PREMISE

1. Why do you want to write this book? What appeals to you about it?
2. What makes it different from other books you've read or heard about?
3. Who is your main character (or characters)? (You don't need to know exactly; this is just a preliminary exercise.)
4. What's the story question? Why would a reader want to keep reading? What's at stake?
5. Do you have a vague idea how it ends?
6. Do you have a message or a theme you want to explore with this book?

7. What do you want the reader to walk away with after reading this book?

Now, those last two questions in particular may seem a little "New Age" or "out there." You just want to write a story, sell it, and have lots of people read it. You might not necessarily care if they walk away with anything other than a few laughs and some stress relief. (And yes, that's a perfectly good reason for anyone to write a book.) And you might not want a theme for your book. I've discovered that most of the time, the theme I thought I was tackling when I wrote a book and the theme that wound up in the final product were completely different animals.

Having said that, I also think that most authors write books because they desperately want to communicate with their readers. There's some experience, some feeling that they want to share with other people. That, generally, is your theme. Most authors work with only a few themes in the course of their entire careers, with each book being a different exploration, a different facet, a variation. Jennifer Crusie, for example, writes books that are about women discovering and accepting themselves. (Most Chick Lit explores some aspect of that theme, actually.) Marian Keyes takes the theme a step further, by showing women who self-destruct and then come out on the other side of enlightenment. Other authors explore issues of friendship and love overcoming obstacles. In my work, I focus on people who need to fight and personally stand up to their worst fears in order to live the lives they really want.

Another thing to watch for: right next to "high-concept," the next dreaded description of a story idea is "breakout," popularized by Donald Maass's book *Writing the Breakout Novel*, which in and of itself isn't a bad little writing manual. The problem is everyone is trying to find the magic formula for the story idea that's going to be "larger than life" and is going to bring fame, fortune, and a one-way ticket to the *New York Times* Best Seller List. They're looking for something hot, something that's going to sell. Breaking out is the "golden ticket" of our industry.

BREAKING OUT VERSUS BREAKING IN

Very few first novels break out. There are plenty that do—*The Nanny Diaries*, for example—but it's not the norm. Breakout books usually happen after a writer has spent several years getting published, honing her craft, and discovering what she's best at . . . then amping it up to the point where a book is an undeniable bestseller. It's sales numbers that determine whether a book is a breakout or not.

Most unpublished authors are much more concerned with breaking *in* to the publishing world. And many of them are willing to sign almost any devil's bargain to get their foot in the door. They pore through Internet listings and loops, trying to learn what editors are hungry for, and whip out proposals that will fit that mold. If they can just strike while the iron's hot, they can get a contract, and then write books that *they* like (since, hey, once you've got a foot in the door, it's not like they can toss you right out, right?) and then have the magical breakout book ensue.

Having been on that side (every published author was unpublished once!) I can understand that desire. However, having been published a while, I also know just how dangerous it is. There are a lot of good ideas out there. There are a lot of shortcuts. Yes, if vampire Chick Lit is hot right now and you know you can write a fairly decent one, you could get your foot in the door that way. You could sell a book. And, if you're a decent writer, you might even get some respectable sales numbers and germinate a career.

But there are some traps they don't tell you about. The first is pigeonholing. You wrote an okay book on something you didn't really love to break in . . . but the publishing industry is going to want you to write more of the same, only different. And they're going to be watching your sales numbers like pilots watching the instrument panel in a cockpit. That's not to say that once you're published, you're chained into just one type of book for the rest of your life. That is to say, you'd better be ready for an uphill fight if you want to jump around. Either that, or they'll convince you to keep writing these books you're not crazy about until you make so much money that they'll publish anything you put on paper. It's a crapshoot, but it's easy to get lulled into that sense of confidence.

The other trap: you're going to miss the wave. You don't necessarily want to write for something that's "hot right now." Yes, publishers may be looking for a certain kind of book, and maybe you're a fast writer who can crank out what they're looking for. If you want to do that, go for it, and there's really no judgment there. It's a good way to make a living doing something that most people only dream of, and if you're having fun, definitely pursue it. However, for a lot of authors I know (and this is going to sound weird), *writing isn't fun*. It beats the hell out of any other job they've ever had, but it's still a process of sweating blood, of forcing yourself to sit in front of your computer on a daily basis. There have been days when my best friends have offered to lash me to my chair and handcuff me to my keyboard tray. And believe me, I've considered taking them up on it.

If you're going to be torturing yourself, it may as well be for something you're going to feel proud to publicize in nine to twelve months.

The last trap: to my knowledge, nobody breaks out with a knockoff. I don't care how high-concept you are, if the publishing industry is noticing that something is "hot," that means that other authors are making a lot of money with something that lots of readers recognize. So they're looking for profitable knockoffs. But unless you're really in love with whatever they're looking for, unless you've been working your butt off on a story that just happens to fit within their scope *and* you're able to figure out what makes your book different . . . you're not going to break out. Instead, you're going to get swallowed whole, and your chances of success are marginal. You're going to be "the next (insert already successful author name here)," instead of the first *you*.

Okay, off the soapbox. Bottom line: make sure you've got a story, not a cool idea. Make sure that you know why you're writing the book. And then get ready to take the plunge.

6.

From Ducklings to Divas

Characters

There's an old chestnut that there are two kind of stories: *plot-driven* and *character-driven*. Plot-driven stories are full of twists and turns and rely on the construct of what happens (and on making sure that plenty of stuff happens, period) rather than who the people acting out the story are. A popular example: James Bond. He doesn't really change much from the beginning of any movie or book to the end. However, lots of neat stuff happens.

Character-driven stories are stories in which the characters themselves are the key to keeping the pages turning. As the reader, you care about the protagonist (generally defined as the main character, who goes through a series of life-defining changes and is different at the end of the book than he/she was in the beginning of it) and you want to see what happens to this person you're learning so much about. You grow close to the character and his/her friends. You want to know more.

Chick Lit and other types of women's fiction are generally considered character-driven. Women readers are presumably more interested in what people are like, who they really are, rather than seeing static characters in situations that are imposed on them. Women or men, today's audience (and by that, I mean anyone searching to be entertained, whether by book, movie, television show, or video game) is looking for more complex, character-driven fare. If readers don't care about your novel, when the ultimate climax of your book happens, when your protagonist is in the worst moment of his/her life, your reader will be bored senseless, or worse, they'll be rooting for your protagonist to get crushed. When I watched *The Blair Witch Project* after much hype, I remember turning to my best friend and saying, "You know something? I hope she dies, because she's annoying the hell out of me."

In Chick Lit, more than almost any other genre, a book can get by on the sheer personality of its main heroine (or heroines). The unsinkable Bridget Jones, with all her tics and flaws, is a perfect case in point. The story is familiar—it's not even all that unique, a simple retread of Jane Austen's classic *Pride and Prejudice*. But Bridget is an endearing, very sympathetic, very *empathetic* character, who was perfect for her time period. She might not be someone you want as a role model, but she would probably be the person you giggled with in the back of a crowded staff meeting. The success or failure of your Chick Lit novel is going to hinge on the main character, so think very carefully about how you're going to create her.

I'm not saying that plot isn't important at all—far from it. I think that novels need to be both character- *and* plot-driven. That is to say, if you've got compelling characters and they're doing things that are both true to their characteristics *and* interesting, with gradually growing stakes, well, then you've got yourself a winner. The thing is, it's really not that easy. If it were, everybody would do it. At least, I hope they would.

So, if you want to create a plot that's tight and compelling, you're going to need a character that the reader will be interested in and that has a lot to lose, one that the reader can actually relate to.

CREATING INTERESTING MAIN CHARACTERS

How to start? If you had a picture of an interesting character in mind when you first developed your premise, then you're a jump ahead. You're going to need to know as much as possible about this character. I'm a big fan of doing character "prewriting." I know . . . it's time-consuming, and technically, you never "see" any of that writing in the novel. Think of it as background work. Trust me, it does pay off once you start writing the novel.

Robert J. Ray has a fantastic book called *The Weekend Novelist.* In it, he includes a character description sheet, a questionnaire really, that helps you get some background on who your character is. It asks basic questions, including physical description (height, weight, eye color, hair color). The exercise I always find fascinating is the one where you describe the character's house. It's a psychological trick: your house describes more about you than you realize. When you write a paragraph on the character's home, you're going to get a sense of who the character is. You may not be able to say baldly, "I see my protagonist as the kind of woman who hates being part of a crowd and would never consider herself cool or materialistic, but who deep down wants to fit in." And even if you did, you don't want to share those characteristics in one sentence with your reader. When you create the home description, you're able to hint at your character and infuse the story with the details instead of force-feeding it in several heavy-handed paragraphs. For example, the woman described above might have deliberately clunky shoes in her closet, nothing fashionable or stylish . . . but she also has expensive mineral water that she rebottles in her environmentally friendly blue plastic water container. She has logo T-shirts but never wears them because they got too popular, and because she doesn't like people staring at her chest. She has a community newsletter with dance classes circled. It's several months old, but it's still on her kitchen counter.

Have fun with the description. It's like a Rorschach test . . . you'll be able to figure it out later, after it digests for a little while. Right now, you're just going for impressions.

Once you determine those sort of background details about your character, you'll want to do a chronology, or a life story, if you want to sound less scientific. This exercise is also in Ray's *Weekend Novelist*. I like to write it out like a mini-story.

"My protagonist, Kelly England, was born in 1973 to Charles and Madelyne England, in a small hospital in East Roanoke, Tennessee. . . ."

From there, I hit what I can think of as the high points, trying to keep in mind what sort of a person I think my protagonist (in this fictitious case, Kelly England) is, how she thinks, what her fears are. Things pop up. Because of the nature of Chick Lit novels, I tend to focus on what my protagonist's relationships are with her family, her friends/cliques/social circle, and her love life. Does she like her parents? When was the first time they punished her, and for what?

Who are her friends? Does she make friends easily or not? Does she have any close friends? When was her first kiss? How old was she when she first had sex? How many boyfriends has she had? Has she ever gotten married? I sketch out the details of when these events took place, what happened, and how they affected her.

Keep in mind—this is also the perfect way to dodge actually writing, so I wouldn't make the chronology more than five pages, max. You're not writing a fictional biography here. You're doing a background check.

Also keep in mind—this is fluid. Think of yourself as a detective. You might think you know a character, but then you'll be writing, and bam! A new revelation, something your research didn't reveal. You've got to be flexible. These documents—the character questionnaire, the home description exercise, the chronology—are just guideposts. They're not set in stone.

The thing is, the more detail you have, the more well-rounded your character will be. Cliché characters, stock characters, two-dimensional characters . . . that comes from an author being lazy and writing down details without much thought. If your character is a giggling "spendaholic" who has a passion for fashion, then it's going to be easy for you to write that and make people think of every other Chick Lit that they've read that had a retail-therapy fashionista as the lead. But if you can take this almost iconic character and give us background on why she is the way she is, what makes her different, what makes her tick, and most important, *why we should care about her*, then, even though the story's familiar and "it's all been told before," people will still keep turning the pages.

Using the fictitious example of Kelly England again, let's say she's the spendaholic. How do we make her different? I don't mean just moving her, although a high-fashion spender in, say, North

Dakota would be an interesting twist—someone who is racking up a fortune on her credit cards, buying designer stuff on-line, only to have nowhere to wear it. That's still an external factor, though, and we're focusing on internal. So, let's say she's in a big city, just like any traditional Chick Lit heroine might be. Why should we care?

Maybe she's spending money to get even with someone—she's using her cheating ex-husband's credit cards and trying to exact revenge via Dolce & Gabbana. Or maybe she's going to die in six months, and she had a list of things to do that included cleaning out Versace. (I wouldn't necessarily equate terminal illness with instant sympathy, however. Still, at this stage, be open to anything.) Maybe she's trying to force herself into bankruptcy, because she knows she can't afford to pay off the school loans she racked up for law school and her private law practice is going under . . . she thinks she can resell whatever she's buying on eBay for a profit afterward. I'd come up with a list of twenty things that make your character different from the ones you've read about, if you're worried about being unique. And no, you can't say, "Most heroines are blond, but mine's a redhead." Come on, now!

That comment does bring up a point: your characters, and your story, can't merely be different by degrees. To really stand out, you're going to need to make some radical departures. Take some risks. Emphasize things. You can always rein in characters once they're on paper. It's really, really difficult to turn up the volume on a meek character, or to flesh out a stock character once she's taken center stage.

BEWARE THE FUN STUFF ...
SECONDARY CHARACTERS

One of my all-time favorite television shows is HBO's *Entourage*. In its second season, it started getting tremendous buzz, partially because the writing staff changed and they introduced a more dramatic character arc, but also because of one actor. Is it the lead actor? One of the principals? The hunky guy whose "entourage" of star hangers-on is the reason for the title?

Nope. It was Jeremy Piven, who played the outrageous agent Ari Gold. A brilliant and gifted character actor, Jeremy stole the show every second he was on-screen. In the second season, he was nominated for an Emmy, and the show's Web site was plastered with his trademark tagline on how men should resolve their differences: "Hug it out, bitch!"

I love Jeremy Piven. For that matter, I adore secondary characters. Here's the problem, though . . . they have the potential to derail your story, to take the thing over and leave you sitting there with your protagonist, whose journey is supposed to be the engine driving the book. Secondary characters usually lack a lot of the angst and baggage that encumber your protagonist. They're less fleshed out, so they have the freedom to be outrageous. And they're a lot of fun. You let yourself go with secondary characters, enjoying the lack of strictures. Suddenly, you find yourself saving all your best bits of banter and your zinging one-liners for your favorite secondary. You save scenes with your secondary for the end of your writing day, because they're your favorite ones to write. When the book comes out, people have little to say about the story itself, but everybody raves about your secondary, which doesn't surprise you.

Then, you try to write a sequel with your secondary as a primary . . . and all hell breaks loose. It's clunky. It's choppy. And, lo and behold, another secondary character suddenly shows up, and your prior "favorite" is now sulking and despondent as you start up a whole new love affair.

And that's exactly what it is. Secondary characters, while fun and very important elements of the plot, are flings. Your marriage has to be with your protagonist, or the story will be imminently forgettable . . . except for those moments with your secondary characters, which will sparkle like diamonds set in lead.

VILLAINS, ANTAGONISTS, AND OTHER MAIN CHARACTERS

If you're planning on writing an ensemble book with several main characters, if you've got a story where an antagonist or villain plays a major part, if you've got any character who you think is going to materially affect your protagonist, you're going to need to do the same background research on them, as well. Especially if you're writing an ensemble book. The background on the antagonist/villain may not need to be as extensive, but how many times have you read a book where the bad guy seems like a prop, something out of a bad movie? Like the stock evil boss in an office politics Chick Lit, or the conniving ex-girlfriend trying to steal the protagonist's boyfriend, the one who is inevitably far too pretty and thin to be trusted. You're not sure why they're so evil, what possible motivation they might have . . . but you do know that, inexplicably, they have it in for the protagonist. Of course, when it's entertaining, or if you're looking for a light read, you might not care. But it's the truly interesting and multidimensional villains that keep you hooked and really up the ante. Those are the books you remember, the ones you loan to your friends with the express promise that they give the book *back* when they're done.

This does not mean that every evil boss needs to have a "soft side" by raising orphaned puppies, or that every ex-girlfriend needs to show that she was abused as a child. But it does mean that you need to know more about them—and they need to have solid reasons for doing what they do. Take the ex-girlfriend scenario. If you know that she was coddled all her life, that she was given absolutely everything because she was sickly as a child, then you'll be able to see why she has no choice but to throw a tantrum and target the pro- tagonist, who she sees as "the person stealing my toys." One of the best examples I've ever seen of this is in Marian Keyes's *Last Chance Saloon*. Tess's wretched boyfriend treats her terribly, but from his point of view, you can see why he thinks he's justified. Even with his reasons, you know that he's not—and you can see how messed up he is. However, it makes him much more three-dimensional. And you can hate him with a lot more passion, rather than just thinking, "Ugh, here's the bad guy, I guess I'll hate him." That's the sort of character that has juice.

Once you've got your cast of characters fleshed out and done your homework, you're ready for the next step: putting them onstage and giving them a script to read from.

7.

There's a Story
in Here Somewhere

Plot

Remember what I said, about plot-driven versus character-driven stories? Well, with any luck, you've got a really solid main character (or multiple main characters, for that matter. I like to have three rotating point of view [POV] characters myself). Now that you've got fascinating people, you've got to put them in an interesting situation. That's where plot comes in.

Some people might think that this chapter is less important than the previous one—that as long as you have interesting characters and funny dialogue, you're going to be fine. Or if the writing is stellar, you're going to be fine. There are plenty of "Chick Literary" books, novels that straddle the line between Chick Lit or commercial fiction and Lit Fict, or literary/noncommercial fiction. A prime example of this is Melissa Bank's *The Girls' Guide to Hunting and Fishing*. The novel is really more of a collection of short stories, told from different viewpoints, with no through line or overall story arc. Other books have taken a page out of that playbook—maybe not in the short-story anthology format, but by focusing more on the writing than on the structure of the novel, knowing that where the character goes isn't as important as the way it's written.

There are also stories that are really just a series of vignettes, strung together—mini-adventures, meant to showcase the characters that you've (hopefully) fallen in love with. Any traditional Chick Lit that poses an overall story arc of "main character's search for love in all the wrong places" will have a very simple plot: girl looks for love, girl finds variations of "wrong" love, girl finally meets love. While the vignettes can seem repetitive, it's *how* the vignette is written that's important. In the Shopaholic series, the main character, Rebecca Bloom, does not change radically. In whatever continent or whatever context, she's first and foremost a shopaholic. But the readers love her for that—and her continuing misadventures in the personal finance arena are what keep them coming back for more. This can work, as well—but you have to make sure that your character is beyond compelling, that she strikes a chord with readers. It's not impossible—obviously, it can be done.

In *Story,* Robert McKee postulates that as a general rule, people love traditional three-act structure stories. It's what we're familiar with . . . how we're geared, as it were. The easiest way for us to identify with a character is to give that character a big, relatable goal. Then, throw an escalating conflict in the way of that goal. Have a climax, where all looks lost—where the absolute worst that you can think of, *in terms of that goal,* happens to your main character. Then, everything gets resolved through actions that the character performs as a result of the changes he's undergone through the course of his journey. Sounds formulaic, but it's like a sonnet. You have the format set, but all the content is wide open. And as formulaic as it sounds, *it works like gangbusters*. Done properly, you can write a big book that people will devour in hours. You'll write a page-turner. You'll have people good-naturedly cursing you at work, when they're exhausted because they stayed up way too late finishing your latest novel. That's your goal.

And how you do that is plot.

SCHEMING AND PLOTTING

If you followed the advice of the last chapter, you should know your characters, at least as well as you can know them before you actually start the rough draft. If you started with a situation instead of a character, then here's how you'll start.

Say you know you wanted to write a book about someone vying for an *American Idol*–esque prize on TV. That's the premise you started off with, rather than the character. You knew that you wanted to write about the dark side of reality shows, and you wanted to write a story with a naïve character that became a streetwise musician at the end of the book. That's a start: you have a theme and a message. So you choose your character—we'll use the fictitious Kelly England again. Kelly's goal, in this case, is obvious. She wants to win the prize. The key here is, *why?* As actors say, what's her motivation?

Motivation is the key to reader empathy. Your reader may hate reality shows, her skin may crawl at the idea of singing in public. But if Kelly has a stellar reason for wanting what she wants, whether the reader agrees with the end result or not, she'll not only go along for the ride, she'll be rooting for your main character every page of the way. If she needs the money because she's going to be evicted, that's easy to relate to—everybody's been broke or afraid of being broke at one point or another. If Kelly comes from a poor family, that makes sense as well. Or what if Kelly comes from a rich family, and she has five siblings, all smarter, more talented, with better jobs? Who hasn't felt overshadowed by someone, or wanted to be recognized for being unique and special? Again—relatable motivation.

Of course, the situation had a clear goal. If you had a premise that was built on a quirky, fascinating character, then the goal might not be as obvious. Say you wanted to write a story about a woman who has been mute all her life . . . not deaf, mind you, only mute. She looks like the most nondescript person on the face of the earth: average height, average weight, shoulder-length hair that's an indiscriminate brownish-blond. She's the human equivalent of the DMV. In fact, she's so ordinary, she's remarkable. That's the story you want to write.

Interesting premise . . . but not a story. Why? Because, once the reader thinks, "Well, that's kind of interesting," unless she is given a reason to invest time in this character, she's going to go wander off and see what's on television. The answer to this: *give her a goal,* something she wants that she doesn't have . . . and something that would be difficult for her to achieve. In this case, she wants to talk. Or . . . *she wants to win an* American Idol–*type reality show.*

Okay. Now you're on to something. Then you can follow up with motivation. Why does she want this goal? And most important, why *now*? Has she always wanted this goal? If so, why are you starting the story when she's an adult, and not a child? Something had to have changed.

Finally, make it a goal that the character can conceivably achieve. Anything's possible . . . but if you took our mute girl and gave her the goal of being president of the United States with no prior political training, it'd be harder for the reader to get over the "oh, come *on* now" factor. Giving her the goal of being a local assemblyperson or even a senator is a little more plausible.

Once you've got the goal and motivation straightened out, you'll be ready to start doing what any good author does: making life difficult for your character. Which brings us to the third necessary point in the "holy triumvirate" of plotting—conflict.

You've got a character you've done a ton of research on. That character has a goal, a big one. She's got a damned good reason for wanting whatever she wants.

So what if, *poof!* She suddenly has exactly what she wants on page twenty?

You've got no story, that's what. And you'll have a reader going, "Er . . . that's nice," and then grabbing the remote.

That's where conflict comes in. In the case of our mute girl, depending on whether her muteness is physiological or psychological, she's got a big set of hurdles. If it's physiological, maybe it means a lot of operations or training or whatever. If it's psychological, you've got to have in your character notes *why* she's mute—what trauma put her in that state. Or maybe it wasn't a trauma. Maybe, in her large family of super-talented siblings, in an ultra-rich household where her parents were never around, she just decided at age seven to stop talking . . . and hasn't spoken since, despite threats, counseling, the punishment of a team of nannies. She just hasn't spoken. She's been waiting for her parents to ask her to, maybe . . . and they never have. They don't even like to be in the same room with her. Flashy and flamboyant, entertainment people, they're utterly self-absorbed. Her father is producing a rival reality show. So her wanting to win is a sort of punishment of some sort, a way to finally get his attention, since nothing else has worked. But her whole life is working against that goal. She hasn't spoken. Her voice would be all tweaked, rusty. She has never sung since childhood. And she's got a natural aversion to the entertainment industry.

This particular plot may not be workable, but you see the point: a big goal, a good reason, and lots of obstacles to be overcome. The goal is the bait, motivation the hook, and conflict the line that reels them in.

For further clarification, you might want to read Debra Dixon's *Goal, Motivation and Conflict*. She covers these points in exhaustive detail, with tons of examples and a pretty nifty little diagram/table. She also covers an important point—*external* goal versus *internal* goal. Let's make Kelly England our mute girl. If Kelly's *external* goal is to win the singing reality show because she wants to destroy her father's show, the conflict is she's been mute since she was seven. But what does she want, internally, subconsciously, emotionally? Her *internal* goal would be that she wants to be recognized and loved by her family. But every child wants to be loved, at any age. What's her conflict? Well, one, they're self-absorbed twits—financial destruction may not help that. Secondly, and from a more pop-psychological standpoint, if she waits for them to recognize her instead of building her own life, she'll always be stunted . . . she'll always be mute.

To really generate some sparks, you want the external goal and internal goal to conflict in some way. So, instead of having an internal goal of wanting to be recognized, what if her internal goal is to disappear entirely? After all, her entire life has not been spent trying to get her parents' attention, it's been trying to see if they'd notice if she were gone altogether, seeing if her extreme behavior would somehow goose them into taking action. Is there some way to bridge the gap? For example, if she does this extreme thing, she'll get her trust fund money, plus the winnings . . . and she plans on changing her name and moving to some remote island, so she'll be able to be mute for the rest of her life without anyone judging her. So, to achieve her goal of being invisible, she has to be very, very visible first.

The key here is to amp up the conflict to the point where the reader actually squirms . . . but keeps reading.

You're going to be going through a lot of permutations. There's a lot of trial and error involved. Still, it's a lot easier to do this kind of brainstorming *before* you go through a few reams of drafts. Drafts are the only thing that can prove these ideas are roadworthy, but this will help you get your ducks in a row. Keep fiddling with the possibilities, and then, when you've settled on a working goal, motivation, and conflict, both conscious and subconscious, write it down and pin it up somewhere visible, near your writing area, or in your notebook if you write in various locations. This is going to be your touchstone—the key to your whole book.

BUILDING THE FOUNDATION IN THREE ACTS

When I was first published, I sold a completed manuscript, a romance novel. The publisher was happy with it. Happy enough, in fact, that they asked for another book, as soon as I had one. Of course, I didn't have another completed manuscript that was in any kind of shape—the only other one I'd finished had already been summarily rejected. So I sold my next book, as most published authors do, on proposal. I had three chapters and a rough synopsis. They said go ahead, complete it in six months.

Considering I also had a day job and a life, in addition to need-ing to complete this novel in six months, I promptly panicked. I also developed the plotting system that I still use today, after six novels and a handful of short stories. It's a template. It's horribly compul-sive, almost scientific in its procedure. But I have to say, despite all this, it works. You don't need to follow it directly, but it does give you a sketchy guide on how to plot a whole novel.

You've got a character with a goal, motivation, and conflict. The goal is the key, the spine of your novel. Absolutely everything (and yes, I mean *everything*) your character does in this novel is going to tie back to either the conscious or subconscious goal in some way.

Now—you write plot points.

In *The Weekend Novelist*, Robert J. Ray has a diagram explain-ing the progression of how three-act structure works. Robert McKee covers it to a certain extent, too, in his book *Story*. In a nut-shell, here's how three-act structure works.

Act one: This is the setup. It leads to plot point one, which is the "glue" that sets your character on the path of no return, propelling her into the hunt for whatever goal she has.

Act two: The big one, the middle. This is the main battleground, the skirmishes that make up the war. There's usually one reversal in-volved in this, the midpoint or plot point two. If plot point one was upbeat, the midpoint is usually downbeat, and vice versa. It ends with plot point three—the calm before the storm—and the setup for the third act, when all hell should (in theory) break loose.

Act three: This is the final battle. The key scene here is what ro-mance writers call the "black moment," when the absolute worst thing that could happen to the main character—*in terms of the char-acter's goal*—happens in spades. Big things happen. Then the char-acter, who has changed, grown, and learned over the course of the first two acts, makes a momentous decision, leading to the climax . . . the big decision. Either the external, conscious goal is achieved through a final act, or the internal, subconscious, true goal of the character is achieved, all to the ultimate satisfaction of the reader. Finally, there's a resolution to help the reader "come down" from the "high" of the climax. The reader puts down your book and waits breathlessly for your next one.

Sounds easy enough, right?

To make it easier, I look at the character's goal sheet, and then I fill out the plot points. I may not know exactly what's going to happen, but I know what I need to shoot for, from beginning to end.

THE PLOT POINTS

1. *The inciting incident.* Robert McKee calls this "the moment that something changes." This is where you start your story. It should be an incident that is unusual for the protagonist . . . something that forces the protagonist to *take an action.* It's also what sets the stage for the goal.
2. *Plot point one.* This is where the conscious goal is stated very clearly, and all the elements are set up. You'll have what the character wants, why she wants it, and why she can't have it (what's standing in her way).
3. *Plot point two (or midpoint).* This is a reversal of the first plot point. If your character decided she had to win the reality show, say, this is where either a doctor tells her she can't talk . . . or she can talk, but she can't sing. Or she sings, and it's a complete disaster, but she makes it further in the competition because the reality show producers

know she'll be a "very telegenic, very marketable freak. Just what viewers want."

4. *Plot point three.* Here's the windup for all the drama in the third act. You need a scene that encapsulates something positive, something that gives the protagonist hope that she can achieve her goal. At the same time, you'll want some reinforcement of why your character can't just walk away from her goal. She's got to be locked onto the path of no return. (You're going to be continually raising the stakes throughout the book, incidentally. More on that in the next chapter.)

5. *The "black moment."* Whatever the conscious and subconscious goal is for your protagonist, this has got to be the absolute worst thing that could happen in the context of that goal. In the case of our mute *Idol* wannabe, the worst thing could be that she loses the competition, that she's a laughingstock on national television, and her parents disavow any relationship to her. Or, it could be one of those twists where she gets what she wants, only to discover that she didn't want it. Say she wins the competition, but she's hounded by the press (unable to make herself invisible) and their angle is: mute-for-years singer gets revenge on unfeeling entertainment-industry parents. She now has her parents' attention, but she's seen as evil, and she feels guilty because her father goes bankrupt as his own show's ratings tank. Or, in option three, she wins the competition, and her parents don't even notice or care, having moved on to another project. They're stunned, but still self-absorbed. All her work has been for nothing.

Whatever happens in this plot point, it's one of your most important. This has got to pack a wallop. At the same time, be careful not to dig a hole your character is unable to climb out of. You've got to wrap this thing up believably, and for Chick Lit, you'll want to end it on a high note, something uplifting. Which brings us to . . .

6. **Resolution.** There's nothing a reader likes better than seeing wrong situations righted, and nothing should be more "wrong" than your last plot point, so here's where you make things better, in a believable fashion. Let me repeat that: *believable.* The Greeks have a term, which was translated in Latin to *deus ex machina*, meaning "a god from a machine." Back in the day, when an ancient Greek playwright wrote himself into a corner, he'd have a guy, this "random god," fly out of the rafters and "save" the hero or heroine, and everyone would live happily ever after. That sort of thing does not play now, obviously, and readers can get really ticked off if you try. That anger translates into "I'll never buy another book from this author again." It also translates into "and I'll tell all my friends how bad this book is." Trust me, this is not the route you want to go. The ending is even more crucial than the black moment, because it's what sells your next book. This is your pièce de résistance, your money shot. This one has got to count. At the same time, it's got to match your character and what she's learned along the way.

Now that you know what the plot points are, you just need to fill them in. Keep them to a sentence or so, for now. Odds are good they'll change once you get into draft form. Besides, this is just a rough sketch, not a blueprint. We'll get into blueprints in the next chapter.

PLOT POINTS:
1. Inciting incident
2. Plot point one
3. Plot point two/midpoint
4. Plot point three
5. "Black moment"
6. Resolution

8.

Driving with a Map

Outlining

As I've mentioned already, I'm compulsive. Remember that six-month deadline I got for the second book I'd ever sold? I had a synopsis, sure, and a rough idea of where I wanted to go. But I had limited time, and I was in no way sure that I could do what they wanted me to do . . . namely, get a certain number of pages done in a certain time frame and have it be any kind of coherent story. I needed a system in a hurry. I'd already sketched out rough plot points, because that's how I wrote the synopsis. (More on the joys and agonies of synopses in Chapter 16.) The problem was how to fit the plot points into a game plan that made sense.

I'd heard a lot of writers speak over the years, and I'm afraid I can't remember which one told me this, but someone relatively fa-mous told me that all major plot points happen, with almost mathematical precision, at the quarter point, half point, and three-quarter point of any book. That person also pointed out that most writers don't even plan for that to happen, it just breaks down that way naturally. Well, I didn't have time to be natural. And like I said . . . I'm way, *way* compulsive.

The system I'm about to describe is not one I'd necessarily recommend most people use. In fact, I imagine most people will look it over and either laugh hysterically or run away screaming. (I have a vivid imagination.) The thing is, again, the system works . . . for me. And I've taught this system to students for years. While few of them actually go to the same lengths (or if they do, they haven't mentioned it to me), just about all of them have been able to glean something useful from the process, whether it's how to outline, how to create an escalating plot, or how to schedule writing to a deadline.

CATHY'S INSANE GUIDE TO OUTLINING

Do the math. When you look at writing guidelines for various publishing houses, they don't tell you page counts, they tell you word counts. A standard-sized Chick Lit novel will be roughly between 95,000 and 110,000 words. What does that mean? As a rough standard, calculate 250 words per page. So a standard novel is between 380 and 440 pages. Generally, I'd say aim for the lower end of the word count. You can always add things if you have to, because cutting things can feel like amputation. I generally pick a target page count of about 400. It's a nice, round number.

If the first three major plot points happen at approximately one quarter of the way apart from each other, that means you need to have plot point one nailed by page 100, the midpoint by 200, and plot point three by 300 at the latest. A lot happens in that last hundred pages.

I also tend to decide around how many chapters I'm going to want to write—a number easily divisible by four, incidentally. I usually write about twenty chapters. If I'm writing 400 pages, that means about twenty pages per chapter. Nice and easy. I have been writing enough to know that I like relatively short scenes, and about three per chapter. Twenty doesn't divide cleanly by three, so I put it between six and seven pages per scene.

If you're the type of person who writes by the seat of her pants, I imagine this whole thing seems pretty baffling to you. How do I know how many chapters I'm going to have? How do I know how many pages, how many scenes? *I don't even know what the story's about yet!*

Again, think of it like a sonnet. All I'm doing is coming up with a set of guidelines. If I wind up writing a four-page scene, or sticking five scenes in a chapter, or write twenty-five chapters, that's fine. This is just a pencil sketch. *It's just an outline.* Nobody's married to it. All it does is give a framework, so I'm not wildly writing and then praying that, somehow, I'll hit my target in the required time frame.

For those of you writing to deadline, figure out how many pages you can comfortably write in a day. (Or, if you've got a tight deadline and you're under contract, figure out how many pages you *must* write a day to meet that deadline.) There's nothing like a deadline, incidentally, to act as jumper cables for your creativity. Even if you're not yet under contract, tell someone when you are going to have the book finished . . . someone whom you admire, and/or someone who will give you hell if you don't get it done. Just make sure the deadline is realistic, and give yourself plenty of leeway. Just because you've written fifty pages in one day doesn't mean that every day is going to pan out that way. Give yourself breathing room. If ten pages a day is good enough for Stephen King, it can be good enough for you. Conversely, if you know you sweat blood and still only produce a page a day, *don't fight your instincts*. You can try to push for more, but slowly. Writing's a tough occupation. The "tough love" school of thought is a dangerous one for creatives, since we don't tend to bend. Instead, we snap, and then we get a writer's block the size of Idaho.

Okay. So, you've got a rough idea of how many chapters you're going to write, how many pages per chapter, how many scenes, how many pages per scene. Now, we switch from math to strategy.

"**Tacking.**" The term "tacking" is something that welders use. They want to fuse two pieces of metal together in very long strips. In order to keep the strips together, they "tack" it, by spot welding a few key joints. That's what holds the two pieces together while they're doing the long, arduous task. They don't go from beginning to end.

Remember what I said about plot points being approximately a quarter of the way through? That would mean, in my twenty-chapter book, plot point one would happen, oh, somewhere in chapter five. Do I have an incident in mind for how plot point one works? I should, if I've got my plot points and have written the synopsis. It should be a scene or two to get it across. So I draw a grid full of blank spaces that looks like this:

CHAPTER	SCENE	DESCRIPTION
1 (Inciting incident)	1	
	2	
	3	
2	1	
	2	
	3	

In chapter one, I'll put in the inciting incident . . . how it begins. When I get to chapter five, I'll put plot point one. Chapter ten will have the midpoint. Chapter fifteen, plot point three. And then, arbitrarily at first, I'll pencil in the black moment, climax, and resolution scenes.

What does this do?

It tells me how much space I have to tell my story. And it gives me a rough estimation of how to set up my plot so that things happen logically, things happen with an escalating intensity, and things happen at the correct pace. That's what I mean by tacking. You're just sketching in key pieces that will hold the whole thing together until you have the time to work on all of it.

It also does another thing: it gives my mind a rest, and something to grasp on to. The thought of sitting down and coming up with the entire plot of a novel is so comprehensive, so huge, that it can be enough to have your mind say, "Oh, screw *this*," and then proceed to lock up your creativity like a jailhouse. So this breaks down the plotting process into easily digestible chunks. You don't have to sit down and try to figure out the steps from beginning to end all in one sitting. You just have to figure out what a few chapters look like. When that's done? Then, you just have to plot from the first chapter, which you already kind of know, to the first plot point . . . which you also already have a bead on. Then, take a breather. Talk with friends. Eat some ice cream. And when you're ready, take on the next leg of your journey: head for plot point two.

Trust me. This is much, much simpler. Here's how.

Fill in the blanks. I've said it before, I'll say it again. I am compulsive. An organizational nutcase. I like to have my ducks in a row. So, when I came up with this system, I knew that I wanted to make sure that I had coherent story arcs, that each plot point had higher stakes than the one prior, and that each character was given the same amount of "screen time" in approximately equal proportions (i.e., nobody vanishes for a few chapters and then pops up again randomly). In my first Chick Lit novel, *L.A. Woman*, I had three major characters who each had their own point-of-view scenes. They consequently had their own arcs, their own major goals, motives, and conflicts—all of which had to wrap up neatly.

I agreed to write the novel in about three months. And did I mention I had a day job? (In my defense, I was young . . . foolish . . . easily mislead. Besides, the promise of an earlier publication date "if you can squeeze this in" is enough to make calmer dispositions than mine dizzy with greed and overconfidence.)

In addition to being a nut for organization, I also have an addiction to nonfiction books on how to write. You've seen me reference a few here: *The Weekend Novelist* and *Story,* for example. I'm about to add another one, a book that changed my life (once I figured out what the hell it was saying). That book is *Scene and Structure* by Jack Bickham. As they say in the movie *Beetlejuice,* the thing "reads like stereo instructions." (Incidentally, *Story* isn't exactly the breezy, light-read, how-to manual of the year, either.) But what I gained from *Scene and Structure* is this: each scene needs to have a goal. (Sound familiar?) This goal needs to tie in with your overarching story goal, which, thanks to your character research and plot points, you already know. Each scene goal has to have a motivation. And each scene goal has to end with one thing: a disaster.

Yes, you read that right.

If the character gets what she wants in the scene, then your story pace stops dead by default. Remember when I asked, "What happens if your character reaches her goal in the first twenty pages?" and the answer was the reader going off to watch television? This is the same thing, only on a smaller scale. The reader may still be invested in finding out if your character still achieves her overall story goal, but they're probably thinking, "She's okay for now," which is dangerous. Why? Because that means you've given them a rest stop. They can now put the book down and do something else. The whole point to calling it a "page-turner" is that they *can't* put the book down. They need to find out what happens. No rest stops . . . your book needs to be the Bataan Death March of fiction!

So, according to *Scene and Structure,* the scene must end with one of the following disasters: a flat-out "no"; a "yes, but"; or a "no, and furthermore."

A scene that ends with a "no" means that the character does not get what she wants. She must find another way to get what she wants.

A scene that ends with a "yes, but" means that the character gets what she wants . . . but in getting what she wants, something else bad has happened that is going to create a whole different set of problems. It's the "spinning plates" disaster, where just as she gets one plate spinning, another threatens to come toppling down.

A scene that ends with "no, and furthermore" means that not only does the character not get what she wants, she's also made her entire situation even worse.

In order to see that your plot actually does this, what I recommend is writing a scene outline. I break down each prospective scene in my book into the following format:

CHAPTER 1
<u>Scene 1</u>
POV:
Goal:
Motive:
Conflict:
Disaster:

I do this with every single scene in the book. By doing this, I can see how often a POV character shows up. I can make sure that each scene somehow ties in to the character's overall story goal. I can make sure that each subsequent scene has higher stakes than the one previous, and that I'm not writing "variations on a theme" . . . say, where a protagonist asks someone for something, gets a "no" disaster, then asks someone else for the same thing and gets a very similar "no." Or, worse, asks the same person and gets another gentle "no." That's just repetition, and it'll slow the whole piece down.

Write this format down for your major plot points first, then try out scenes that will get you from one plot point to the next.

By the time you're finished, you will have a complete and fairly comprehensive document that shows the skeleton of your novel. You'll also be grateful that you did all the legwork once you start wrestling with the actual draft (and see the pitfalls that can crop up in that piece of business). Now, all you have to do is flesh it out by your deadline.

9.

Joyriding

Free-form Writing

As a compulsive plotter and planner, I am obviously not a big proponent of "seat of your pants" writing. However, when I first started writing, that's how I worked . . . how we all work, I imagine. There is something to be said for the freedom and sheer creativity of writing blind, of not knowing where you want to go or how the story is going to take form. Characters simply spring out of the ether, funny bits of dialogue pop out of nowhere, and your plot twists and turns in ways you would never imagine. On the negative side, you also meet characters who try to wrestle your book away from you (and make it all about *them*, strangely enough) and you more than likely hit a lot of wrong turns, plot roundabouts, and dead ends. It's both exhilarating and frustrating.

At the same time, I know authors who have broken out in a cold sweat just hearing about the lengths of my outlining. If you're a "pantser," as the term goes, then it's pretty much impossible for you to do anything I mentioned in the previous chapter. And I completely respect you for it.

At the same time, "pantser" or not, there are going to be times when you've got to write to deadline, too. And you probably want to have the same escalating stakes and progressive plotting. You naturally are going to want to write a page-turner.

So, the following tips are what I've gathered from a simple survey of my writing friends who would rather be bound stark naked to a fire-ant hill than write an outline.

Do your research. If you're going to be writing about manning a schooner across the Atlantic, do a bunch of research beforehand. The details will seep into your unconscious, and you'll have, by default, more to write about.

Write fast. Join one of those book-in-a-week or book-in-a-month challenges. Instead of being paralyzed by the potential choices or brooding over the decisions you're making, you're going to be "mainlining" writing from your subconscious, effectively shutting off the stranglehold your internal editor has on your writing. This means a faster first draft.

Write often. As a seat-of-the-pants writer, you're much better off writing regularly. It's all about training your mind to be creative on demand. If you write by outline, you'll know how much you need to get done, and by when . . . and you'll be able to gauge how far behind you're falling. As a pantser, you're not going to have that luxury. Writing daily, and writing a set page count, will help alleviate some of those problems. Even if you're not writing to deadline, it's still a good habit to develop, because it's easy to say, "I'm still thinking of how it's going to work out." While brainstorming and what Lawrence Block calls "creative procrastination" is important, it can easily become a dodge . . . all thinking, no writing. I forget where I picked this up, but one of my favorite quotes is, "writers don't write with their minds, they write with their hands."

Revise, revise, revise. From what I can tell, most pantsers "don't write books, they rewrite books." So, once you've got your first draft done, take a breather and then look it over critically. Find out where it's slow, where it's vague, where a character just doesn't seem believable. Take notes. Then take another pass at it. Repeat as necessary, or until deadline hits.

Read, read, read. There are some really prestigious pantsers out there. Stephen King. Nora Roberts. The list is long and distinguished. And if you read some interviews with these people, you're convinced that they're geniuses. They seem to *know* instinctively how the stories are supposed to run, how to craft a plot twist without any planning, and how to make sure all the little dangling plot lines get neatly knotted at the end, like some kind of divine preordination. While I think in a lot of cases genius is involved, there is another trick to help hone this "plotting instinct." Read voraciously, especially in the genre you're hoping to write. After a lot of exposure, your brain will eventually sublimate the basic structure of what you're hoping to write. You may have to be careful of cliché—and you'll really want to be careful that you didn't, say, sublimate an entire passage or storyline—but you will also have a well-developed sense of how plot ought to work.

Those people who are pantsers who have at least given the outline method a try admit that even a basic outline seems to help increase their productivity and their confidence. Of course, there are also people I know who find outlining an absolute wall to creativity and killjoy in writing. "If I know how it's going to go, I become completely bored with it," a friend of mine told me. So I'd say try outlining once, and if you feel the same way . . . don't do it. The important part here is to enjoy the writing process, and the stories you create. This sounds like New Age "feel-good" hokum to a certain extent, but trust me, you've got years to hate your writing job. Enjoy whatever you can before you have to worry about publishing.

10.

Underwire for Your Novel

Structure

Once you've got the idea of what your story is about and who your story is about, you'll want to decide how to tell your story. This can be a little trickier for Chick Lit than in other commercial genres. Unlike most literary fiction novels, you won't necessarily be following one character and telling her straightforward story. And, unlike a mainstream suspense or adventure novel, you won't be featuring a cast of thousands: the main character, the evil enemy, the poor schmuck in charge of the fatal plutonium who is a starring character for all of five pages. Also, unlike a traditional romance novel, you won't be switching off, he-said/she-said style, between a hero and a heroine. If anything, Chick Lit draws most closely from its women's fiction predecessors. The format is important because, these days, Chick Lit readers look for something a little more unusual. Like voice, style, and commercial hook, your format might become a selling point by the unique way you set up the book.

Here are a few examples of how books are structured and what sort of impact each makes.

Singular protagonist, traditional. This is the traditional: one main character, story told in direct chronological order. This can be told in the first person or the third person, but there is only one point of view (POV). There can be subplots, but the bulk of the story will center on the main character's goal.

Multiple protagonists. This is an ensemble book, which includes multiple "main characters" and more than one POV character. There is a precedent for the multiple protagonist book in women's fiction. Books like Rebecca Wells's *Divine Secrets of the Ya-Ya Sisterhood* or Amy Tan's *The Joy Luck Club* are perfect examples of multiple protagonists and interwoven (yet fairly equally distributed) storylines. Three seems like a good workable number, although if there's a direct conflict, say between a mother and daughter or a woman and her sister, two POV characters work just fine. The best part about multiple protagonists is the fact that the "heavy lifting" is spread evenly over a few characters, so you're not trying to fill four hundred pages with one woman's life. Again, you'll want to make sure that all storylines are given fairly equal treatment, and that no character is introduced only to disappear for half the book and then show up again later . . . unless there's a significant dramatic necessity for it. Another way that multiple characters could be used is in something similar to the film *Rashomon* or William Faulkner's *The Sound and the Fury*: one narrative, told from back-to-back multiple viewpoints. This hasn't been explored as much as it possibly could be in the future.

Linked vignettes/short stories. Again, the short-story-anthology approach. This isn't really a novel, per se, but can act as one. Choose whether you're going to write linked short stories about one character or a series of characters with one common element. In Michael Weinreb's collection *Girl Boy Etc.* there are several stories that examine relationships from largely the male point of view. Sandra Tsing Loh's *A Year in Van Nuys*, on the other hand, is memoir-style nonfiction that parodies *A Year in Provence*. And, of course, the now classic *Sex and the City* does not have a traditional story arc, but instead appears as a collection of adventures happening to the iconic Carrie Bradshaw. This approach seems a bit closer to the literary tradition rather than the commercial genres and can be used to good advantage if you're more interested in showcasing theme (and if you weren't interested in pursuing a traditional story plot, as I suggested in earlier chapters).

Flashback stories. This is a story told in a nonchronological order—things happen, then the character cuts back to previous events. This can be used as a dramatic element, as in Wendy Markham's *Mike, Mike and Me,* in which the protagonist is a woman who dated two men named Mike. The story begins in the present day, where Markham's heroine is married to one of the Mikes, and unfolds in the past. The "mystery" is figuring out which Mike the protagonist ended up with. This is a device that can be confusing, but that also allows for a great deal of creativity. Think of movies such as *Memento,* which is told backward, a device that was also used by author Chuck Palahniuk in his novel *Survivor,* where even the pages are numbered backward. Don't be afraid to experiment.

The "written record" format. I've already cited *Bridget Jones's Diary* as a precedent, and this format is starting to get used to the point of cliché. An entire story told in e-mail trails is the format for

Meggin Cabot's *The Boy Next Door*. Journals of all sorts have also been done. Letter exchanges are especially popular in Young Adult fiction. There have been novels that have been a mishmash of correspondences: e-mails, letters, memos, etc., all pieced together to form a narrative. It can be done . . . but, unfortunately, a lot of it has been.

The "gimmick." In the musical *Gypsy*, the strippers proclaim, "You gotta have a gimmick," and the same thing can be true of Chick Lit. With the glut of Chick Lit novels that were produced after the boom right at the turn of the millennium, it got harder and harder to set your novel apart—to give it the sense of quirkiness that readers would find appealing. This spurred the emergence of "gimmicky" formats—novels with a recipe, a how-to tip, a song, or a guidebook passage. The complete "song list" for various books, such as *Getting Over Jack Wagner*, became something of a value-add for several books. Readers do enjoy some of these features. If your book is something like *A Girl's Guide to One-Night Stands* and your heroine is a freelance writer creating a series of articles based on this, then it makes sense. However, like the "written record" format, this has been done quite a bit. You'll want to make sure that you're aware of what has come before, and have really good reasons for using it now.

11.

Whose Story Is This, Anyway?

Point of View

It all started with Marian Keyes's Chick Lit novel *Watermelon,* in which the protagonist, Claire, speaks directly from her own point of view. The follow-up punch: Bridget Jones's first-person-style diary. From then on, most Chick Lit novels were written in a very conversational first-person account. There have been plenty of deviations since, but beginning Chick Lit writers, or writers who are considering Chick Lit, usually ask me the same thing: "Do I have to write in first person? Do I have to keep using 'I' all the time?"

The answer, in short form, is *no.*

However, it's important to note that the use of first person showed a remarkable break from the romance and women's fiction that preceded Chick Lit. The conversational tone, the humor, and the protagonists' relative self-absorption were a radical departure.

Choosing a point of view is a very important part of writing any sort of novel, and Chick Lit is no exception.

SO WHAT IS POINT OF VIEW?

So we're all on the same page, I'm going to go over what point of view is, the different points of view that exist, and why it's important for you to pay attention to this as a writer.

Point of view is, literally, whose "viewpoint" the story is being told from. (I know . . . *duhhh*. Be patient.) Called POV for short, it is like the framing of camera work in a movie. The POV you choose determines how close the reader can get to the story . . . and what the reader can "see."

FIRST-PERSON POV

First-person POV is a story that's written as if it were being told by the main character. For example: "One day, I was walking down the street, and I couldn't believe it. There was a black Lamborghini just sitting there, with the keys inside. . . ." Because the character is telling you the story, she can interject plenty of personal opinions. ("I thought it was so cool!") There can also be very colorful language choice. ("Then the driver walked up—he was ninety years old and wearing spandex pants. *Spandex*, I tell you. I swear, I wanted to vomit. And then he winked at me! Uh . . . *excuse me!* What did I look like, his nanny?")

The pros of writing in first person: you get very close to the story, and it's very conversational. You know exactly what the main character is seeing, what she's feeling, and what she's going to do, every step of the way. The repetitive use of "I" puts the reader "in the shoes" of the main character, allowing her to identify with the character and live vicariously through her.

The cons of writing in the first person: you are limited to only what the character is seeing and feeling. Thoughts and opinions of people whom the heroine sees around her are completely inaccessible, unless the heroine makes some judgment calls. The protagonist can say, "I saw her, and she looked really angry at me." But you can't share any information that the heroine has no way of knowing, like, "She was angry at me because she'd just found out I was her long-lost sister," if your heroine wasn't present at the meeting where the other character had that revelation. Also, if you're writing in the first person, you'd better make sure that your POV character is very, very compelling. She's going to be the driver for the rest of the book, and if your reader doesn't like her and her voice, you're sunk.

THIRD-PERSON POV

This is the POV most genre novels are traditionally written in. It's told from different characters' POV, although you probably ought to choose one POV per scene. (Not all authors do this—it's certainly not necessary. When done poorly, however, "POV-hopping" or "head-hopping" can be very confusing.) Third person is usually told in the past tense, and it's told as if by a narrator. However, that narrator is limited by the POV character.

If you have two people in a scene, Rick and Jane, and the story is being told from Rick's point of view in the third person, then the scene could go something like this:

> Rick stood outside of Jane's apartment. Jane didn't notice him at first—she was too intent on staring at the black Lamborghini that was parked on the street. Rick himself took public transportation all the time, something he knew that Jane detested. Not that it was keeping him up nights. "Hey, Jane!" he called, finally getting her attention. She smiled, and he suddenly didn't care that she judged his transportation choices.

Notice what's going on there. It describes the scene: Rick is standing outside of Jane's apartment. He sees Jane, but Jane doesn't see him initially. Rick describes the fact that he usually takes public transportation, and then the narrator shares that Rick knows Jane hates that. "Not that it was keeping him up nights" is another view into Rick's emotions and choice—his personality. Yes, it describes Jane, but it isn't Jane's POV. The narrator, for lack of a better term, is firmly on Rick's side and reports only Rick's thoughts and feelings, as well as what Rick's looking at. A friend of mine said that POV is like "a camera set on a character's head. If he can't see something, you can't write about it." So, in this particular case, the narrative can't say, "There was a car three miles away with Rick's friend Steve sitting in it, idling," because Rick can't see three miles away. It also can't say, "Jane was thinking of what a loser Rick was when Rick said, 'Hey, Jane!' and she looked over."

Well, okay, you can. You can do whatever you want. But, like I said, it's a bit confusing.

"DEEP" THIRD-PERSON POV

This is basically third person but with a heavy emphasis on the POV character's thoughts. Usually, thoughts are interjected in italics. This is as close as you'll get to first person without jumping into using "I" all over the place. For example:

> Jane was expecting Rick to come over anytime. Granted, he'd probably take the bus or the subway or something, which meant that he wouldn't be taking her anywhere fancy, since there was nothing fancy in walking distance.
>
> *God, Jane, you're such a snob. Why are you like that?*
>
> She closed her eyes. She'd been castigating herself ever since she started dating Rick . . .

You don't want to overdo it with the mental notes, obviously, but at the same time, "deep" third person lends itself to some funny observations. It also gives a little distance, and you're better able to switch off scenes between various POV characters.

THIRD-PERSON OMNISCIENT

I'm only including this because it *is* a type of POV, even though you don't see it very often in Chick Lit. In this case, the narrator can say things like, "Meanwhile, in a car three miles away . . ." because the narrator knows all, sees all, and isn't aligned with any character in particular. In some cases, the narrator himself becomes a character of sorts. Take the children's series Lemony Snicket: A Series of Unfortunate Events. It's written in the style of a turn-of-the-century writer and captures the series of disasters that befall a set of three orphaned children. The narrator, Mr. Lemony Snicket, can make dire predictions because he knows everything that's going on before any of the main characters do. The POV choice is funny, and it's deliberately stylistic. A Chick Lit example of this: Sarah Mlynowski's novel *Fishbowl* is written in the first person—but with three different POV characters. So while each chapter is written in the first person, using "I" statements, each chapter has one of three different women "speaking." It's a little confusing, but it's also an interesting departure, and it showcases how even when using "I" for three different characters, three different voices can shine through. The funniest "character" is the omniscient narrator, who has his own little chapter-ettes interspersed throughout the book. It's clever—but it might be difficult to sustain throughout an entire novel.

12.

Wherever You Go,
There You Are

Setting

Because I made such a big deal about urban locations and small towns in Part I, I wanted to make sure that I included something on settings in this section. Setting can and should be a character in your book. A story that takes place in Boston is going to be hugely different than one that takes place in San Diego. There's a different vocabulary, different climate, and above all, a different mind-set. Your characters and their backgrounds should either mesh with the setting or grate against it, as in a fish-out-of-water story.

If you're writing about a woman who is trying to change her life but feels like she's trapped, putting her in an environment that reflects that might be a helpful tool. It's a lot easier to believe that a woman is miserable and that fate is conspiring against her when the wind chill is five below zero and she's trying to dig her car out from six feet of snow. If she's in the Florida Keys, watching the sun go down on some beach, it's a little harder to sympathize. On the other hand, if she's a type-A go-getter who had a mental breakdown on the job, watching her crawl the walls in what ought to be a tropical paradise might be a perfect foil to illustrate how people create their own versions of hell. Southern writers have used the communities and environments of the South, with even the slow cadence of their literary voices mimicking the slow drawl and heavy, humid atmosphere of Louisiana, Georgia, and Mississippi.

Setting moves beyond simply the city where the characters act out most of the plot. I have a tendency toward dialogue-heavy novels—they're practically screenplays in early drafts. I am enamored with characters. Years ago, a critique partner pointed out that they were simply talking heads in a vacuum if I didn't pay attention to "anchoring" them in some kind of environment. Beyond that, the environment can "show, not tell" a lot about your characters and what's going on in the scene. Remember that exercise about describing your character's apartment? You can actually use that stuff in much the same way. If your characters are meeting for a regular lunch or brunch, see if you can change it up by shifting the location—a church meeting, a batting cage (à la the movie *When Harry Met Sally*), a white-water rafting trip. Take the time to make the setting integral to the scene.

Having said that, like any secondary character, you don't want the setting to take over the scene—or the novel, for that matter. Don't start each scene with a hefty paragraph of description. Don't go overboard mentioning landmarks and streets to prove your authorial authenticity. ("Look, Ma, I did research!") Although I'd be fascinated to see a novel where the city became a POV character, a lot of other people might not be. Blend it in, don't carpet bomb with it.

13.

Being You and Loving It

Voice

If you've read any other how-to writing books, or heard authors speak or joined any writing organizations, you will at some point hear about "having a distinctive voice." This is, admittedly, an important factor in having commercially saleable writing, in addition to making sure your work is as distinct and "your own" as possible.

What they're never able to explain is how to figure out what your "voice" is. What if you have different voices? What if your voice happens to sound like someone else's? And how are you supposed to develop a voice if your writing seems to lack anything unique?

It can take years. And yes, you can have different voices, to a certain extent, especially if you're writing for more than one genre. Friends of mine who write mystery novels for one publishing house and romantic comedies for another tend to have different voices, rather than writing "funny" mysteries or "edgy" comedies. However, they tend to have elements that make them the same. That's voice.

A distinctive voice is also a very good selling point. It dictates the types of books you write best.

Take for example Jennifer Crusie. She's not a "Chick Lit" author, or at least, she doesn't say she writes Chick Lit. (All Chick Lit authors I know desperately want her affiliated with the genre, though!) She has been writing romantic comedy that has blurred and often broken the boundaries of the romance genre's conventions, and she has the sense of humor that is tailor-made for Chick Lit—even if she foregoes several of the traditional elements ("Chick Lit fabulous" and urban locale, to name a few). Jennifer Crusie has a voice that's distinctive. She writes with deep third-person POV, and she's got an absolutely stellar sense of dialogue. Then, of course, there's her choice of subject matter: zany comedic situations with a naughty, sexy edge to them, as well as female protagonists you'd love to hang out with for coffee.

All those elements make her writing different from the rest.

Stephen King's "voice," on the other hand, is what I call Garrison-Keillor-meets-Edgar-Allan-Poe. It's scary as all get out, from a plot standpoint, or at least "creepy as all get out" until people die. But his writing voice is easy, slow, and almost anecdotal, and very small-town New England in its tone, word choice, and expressions. Most of the time, it's also very funny, a counterpoint again to the horror that's brewing. In fact, it's the dichotomy between his very nonthreatening tone and what's really going on that makes it all the more powerful. If someone overwrites something, all but sticking signposts in it that say, "This is scary!" or, "This is funny!" then it winds up being neither.

In Chick Lit, it's especially important to find your own voice. If you're writing "traditional" Chick Lit, then you're going to be competing with very similar storylines. You're going to need something to help your book stand out, something that will set you apart in the sea of city-set drinks-and-dating-disaster stories. Granted, a unique commercial hook is going to be more useful—we'll get to that more in Part III on selling your novel. But overall, your career is going to depend on showing that your voice and your books are something special.

That something special is going to boil down to your voice.

FINDING YOUR VOICE

So, how do you find your voice?

If you think your voice sounds too much like somebody else's, then you're either reading too much of that author's work and you ought to branch out a little more, or you love that author's work so much that you want to mimic his/her success. The problem is, book buyers already *have* whomever it is you sound like . . . and while I do jones for books when my favorite authors aren't publishing, I'm not willing to buy someone else's book simply because they're "a lot like" or "almost as good"!

You don't want to be the generic version of a bestseller, believe me.

If you've been writing for a few years, this may be painful, but reread your stuff and see if you can be objective enough to mark what really stands out. Consider what you like best about your writing itself, as opposed to the story. Use a highlighter. Mark passages that you think popped. For a Chick Lit writer, humor tends to be an important element . . . not all-important, and not essential, but it's a fairly common aspect of the genre. You might want to highlight anything you thought was funny in its own distinct color. Why? To see what strikes you as personally funny, where the common points are. Maybe you are the queen of funny dialogue. Maybe you have funny opening descriptions. Maybe you have a strange narrator, or you write funny little e-mail snippets, or you can portray slapstick humor in a really brilliant way. *That's* going to be your voice, your best selling point. That's what you should be emphasizing in query letters, synopses, and in your novels themselves.

What if nothing's jumping out at you? What if it all seems . . . *bland*?

Odds are good you've lost perspective. There is a solution—but it's a bit extreme.

THE VOICE-FINDING COMMITTEE

You only want to do this with people you really, really trust. These people don't have to be writers, although they should enjoy reading Chick Lit and understand what's good about it. Get a group of four or five people, if you can. Arm them with highlighters. Then give them samples of your work and have them mark what pops and what's funny.

Do not, under any circumstances, allow them to criticize or critique the work. That is not what this exercise is about at all, and if you've lost perspective, this will be even more damaging. No negatives! No naysayers! When it comes to pessimism, you're fully stocked, so don't add any!

Once they've highlighted what they liked, have them answer a few simple questions:

- What did you like about my writing?
- What do you think I do well?
- What makes me different from other authors you've read?

Once you have their feedback, arm yourself with some comfort food (chocolate and/or mashed potatoes are my weapons of choice) and read what they've written. This should be a feel-good process—nobody should be criticizing—but it's traumatic when other people read your work, especially if you haven't been published yet. (It's still a bit unnerving even when you are published, strangely enough.) So be gentle with yourself throughout this process.

See what kind of overlap shows up. This is why having at least four people is important. If you just get one person to read your work, you're only getting one view. Try to get very different friends to make up your "focus group," too, to ensure the broadest array of responses.

Allow yourself to feel good when you read the compliments your friends write down. It's too easy to say, "Well, they're not writers/not published/not editors," or, "They're my friends, of course they're going to say nice things about me." This is a tough business. If you don't have self-confidence, you're going to get crushed like a bug, and nobody's going to feel bad about it. And a unique voice is basically an assertion of yourself. When you feel the most "you" is when your voice is going to naturally come through.

What happens if their comments are not helpful? By this, I mean comments like, "I loved all of it," or, "Your writing is fresh," or, "Your humor is edgy!" What the heck does fresh and edgy mean? And how can you duplicate it?

First of all: if you're fresh or edgy and you want to keep doing it, odds are good you won't be able to help it (so you won't have to worry about repeating the effect).

Second of all: if they're loving all of it, you probably won't need to worry all that much. Look at what they've highlighted. Unless the pages you got back are a solid block of fluorescent highlighter, you should be able to connect the dots yourself and see what they zeroed in on: dialogue, exposition, or description. See if there's a commonality there.

ALTERNATE EXERCISE: YOUR TRUE VOICE

This is a little weird, but another thing that might help you "find your voice" is listening to your voice . . . literally.

You're a storyteller. Pick one of your favorite anecdotes from your personal life, and then record yourself telling it to a friend. It helps to have a friend physically in the room because you'll be less self-conscious and, with any luck, less aware of the whole "recording" process. The trick is to speak naturally. Tape a couple of hours of conversation, if you need to.

In that conversation, notice when you say something funny. If you tell a story, notice which words you use. I go through phases where I use specific slang and phrases, over and over, until my friends pick it up as well. This is part of your voice, too.

Do you use slang? Any peculiar expressions?

Do you swear? Do you avoid swearing?

When you tell stories, do you have a lot of surrounding setup that's funny, or do you focus strictly on the "and then he was like . . . and then she said . . . and then I . . ." action bits?

Do you make observations about the world in general? Think Seinfeld and his monologues on anything from rental cars to how the ocean is "like a bouncer at a club."

You might go through all of this and still not be able to determine what your voice is. Be patient, keep writing. And don't worry or work at it. As you learn to trust your writing talent, it'll just show up.

PRIMING YOUR VOICE

There is one other little trick I have to add about developing your voice.

When I was writing *L.A. Woman*, I knew that I wanted it to be slightly grittier, even though it is very much a traditional Chick Lit novel. To do this, I loaded my brain with things that I felt would influence my writing.

Have you ever watched a movie, something exciting like a spy movie or a bank heist or something, and then walked out of the theater with your adrenaline pumping, half-pretending in your head, "What would it be like if I were a spy/bank robber/jewel thief?" You can do the same thing to prep for writing. I knew that I wanted a distinctive yet funny voice, with plenty of "edge." To develop that: I watched the movie *Fight Club* a couple times a week while I was writing. I listened to music that I knew would put me in that frame of mind, too—Nine Inch Nails, old Limp Bizkit, the Doors. If you know what influences your mood, it'll influence your book. Use those influences to your advantage.

TELL ME IF YOU'VE HEARD THIS ONE...

One of the defining characteristics of Chick Lit is its humorous tone, whether it's broad slapstick situations or subtle, wry wit. From the urbane to the obscure, humor is completely subjective. It's also, to my mind, impossible to teach. Oh, you can study the mechanics and learn about elements that make things funny, like the structure of telling a joke. You can also learn about setting up expectations, or using comedic contradictions; you can read the best in the business and dissect each turn of phrase. But no one can tell you how to actually *be funny*. You can follow the recipe to the letter but still die on the page, and nobody could tell you what happened.

The thing is, being funny is like being cool—if you're trying to be, odds are good you're not.

So instead, I'd like to reassure you with a couple of things.

You're funnier than you think. If you like Chick Lit, you've probably got a good sense of humor to begin with. Do you like telling jokes to friends? Do they laugh when you tell them? Good, you've probably got a sense of timing. Do you smile when you read your own work? Does your mouth seem to lack an internal censor? Fantastic. This is the one time in life when that's going to come in handy. (As opposed to, say, a job interview, which is when my mouth usually decides to come up with quips.)

You don't need to be all that funny. Chick Lit has a sense of humor, but it doesn't have to. It needs to have attitude, yes. But it doesn't need to be like a stand-up comedian, peppering every other line with "don't you hate . . . ?" and "have you ever noticed . . . ?" Your characters don't have to brandish rapier wit and crush everyone with their Oscar Wilde-esque witticisms. You don't have to be funny. You just have to be *real*. Real beats funny any day of the week.

You can relax. Once you put aside the whole "trying to be funny" business and just focus on writing about what you're feeling, doing some real go-for-the-jugular stuff as well as your own observations on life, you're going to see humor sneaking in whether you mean for it to be there or not. Don't force it. Just let it happen.

14.

Warning: Period of Time When Your Life Will Necessarily Suck

Revisions

There are some authors who feel like their books aren't written, they're *rewritten*. Similar to freeing Michelangelo's *David* from a block of marble, these authors carve away draft after draft until they reach their masterpiece, which they then polish to a high sheen, leaving no word or punctuation mark or page break untouched.

I don't know about you, but people like this make me nuts.

Now, I'm not saying there's anything wrong with people who do this. (Well, let me amend that to say that I think perfectionism is dangerous, and while I'm an insane plotter, even my compulsive habits have their limits.) I just know my own work habits. When it comes to blueprinting and brainstorming a story, I'm in heaven. But when the white-hot fury of the first draft cools down, I look forward to the revision process the same way most people anticipate a firing squad.

Still, no novel is perfect right off the bat. And in today's market, you're going to want to do everything you can to make your manuscript stand out from the rest. If you've got a great story, an editor is not going to turn down your manuscript and pick up a shoddier story simply because that author had the right font, margins, and fewer typos. Revisions aren't just the nitpicky details, however. It's like finishing furniture: you need to do a couple of passes, with gradually finer and finer sand. With revisions, you're going to go to gradually smaller and smaller details.

FIRST: THE COOLING-OFF PERIOD

When you first finish a manuscript, do not, *do not*, DO NOT try and revise it immediately. Why? Because you know it too well, you're too close to it, and you've lost all perspective. Your eyes will glaze over things and your mind will fill in details that may or may not be on the page, simply because it's sick of seeing what you've been working on every day for the past few months. It's too familiar. The trick is to let the project cool down. If you don't trust yourself (and I often don't), it helps to have a friend that you trust "sit" on the manuscript for a few weeks. (Unless you're on a really hideous deadline, a month is a good time frame for cooling off. If you're under a bad time crunch, however, at least give yourself a week.) During the cooling-off period, I'd suggest doing lots of stuff to relax, because writing itself is stressful. That doesn't mean take a month off of writing, however. When you do write, work on a different project. Brainstorm new plot points for something else. Do "writing practice," as outlined by Natalie Goldberg in her writing how-to book *Writing Down the Bones*. Try not to think about the novel you've just completed.

With any luck, when you do get your manuscript back, it won't seem familiar at all. If you're really lucky, you won't remember writing parts of it. Hopefully, this will be a happy thing, like, "I'm better than I thought I was!" However, be prepared for the opposite reaction: "Wait, what the heck was I thinking here?"

ROUGH GRIT REVISIONS: ROUND ONE

When you're ready to dive back in, keep your main character goal sheet next to you, and refresh yourself on the main story goal. Then read your manuscript through, from beginning to end, in one sitting if possible. Take your time—again, it's easy for you to start "skimming" simply because you know what's going on. The trick here is to read it like a reader . . . see if everything makes sense. You're not going to be able to hover over the reader's shoulder and "explain" what's supposed to happen, it all has to come across right there on the page. Read for understandability. Don't look for grammar errors, typos, or anything else "technical." You'll catch that later. The first round is for understandability and pacing. Arm yourself with some Post-it notes. When you find yourself getting bored, or things seem slow, stick one of those bad boys onto the page. You'll figure out what's wrong later. Look for anything that isn't making sense, too. Did you have a plot element in mind that you wound up abandoning . . . but there are references to it later? Did you change a character name halfway through the book, or turn a blonde into a brunette without meaning to? Hit it with a Post-it. Anything that stops you in the reading and makes you go "huh?" is something to flag.

The continuity errors are easy enough to change, so we'll focus on pacing. If a scene seems slow, look at the scenes around it. Did you already have a similar conflict or a similar scene? The pacing may be off because it's too repetitious—it doesn't move the story forward. See if there's a way to either increase the stakes or cut out the scene entirely. If it just doesn't seem to serve a purpose, if it's different, but it doesn't really interest you, ask yourself why. What's going on in the scene? Does it focus on secondary characters who are funny but don't really serve the greater story goal?

If you've outlined the story, hopefully you've already got the scenes set up so that each is subordinate to the overall story goal, and each subsequent scene builds off of the dramatic tension of the one before. Still, you'll want to check each scene at this phase to make sure the pacing is even and to make sure that everything "points the right way," that is, that every scene leads to the final climax. If you've written this without an outline, you'll definitely want to make sure that your stories don't meander too much. Streamlining your plot and pacing is an art, and a skill worth learning.

FINER GRIT: SECOND-ROUND REVISIONS

Once you've got the overall pacing and story continuity covered, you'll want to look at characters. Here's a tricky one: do the major characters sound different and unique? If you just looked at a page of dialogue, could you tell which character was which? And does each scene have POV purity? (Unless you're deliberately "head-hopping" and switching POV's midscene. In that case, read to make sure that your POV-hopping is coherent and the reader can follow where you're leading.)

And let's not overlook setting. Have you anchored each scene in some kind of physical space? I know personally that I have such fun with the dialogue and the characters that, in early drafts, they tend to just pop out of limbo, acting out their scenes in a sort of vacuum. Setting is part of the overall atmosphere. Used properly, it can be a character unto itself, like New York in *Sex and the City*. Beyond that, setting gives important details about what's going on. An argument taking place in a swank, upscale apartment is a much different thing than an argument taking place in the alley behind Tacos Tacos at three thirty in the morning. You don't need to go overboard and start each scene with a page of description. Just make sure that the setting is mentioned and that little details are carefully blended in along the way.

FINAL POLISH: LAST-ROUND REVISIONS

You've got a perfectly paced page-turner with sparkling characters, fun dialogue, intriguing settings. Now, all that's left is the language. This is the part that makes me want to tear my hair out.

You should do a spell check, but keep in mind that homonyms and some typos will still pass through, so read carefully. But the final revision is more than just checking for spelling errors.

Every writer has a few phrases and words that they are abnormally married to . . . a bit of description, or an expression of disbelief. Or, when you're writing, you may just not be paying attention to the fact that you've described somebody's eyes twice in one paragraph. Look for *repetitions*. Circle them in the manuscript. You'll want to edit them. Look for things like adverbs—anything ending in "-ly." Personally, I don't have a problem with them. But they should be deliberate choices. If you've got the time, read some things out loud. See if anything sounds weird or awkward.

Finally, to borrow from Faulkner, there's a phrase in writing called "kill your darlings." That means a sentence that you absolutely love, or a descriptive phrase, or a bit of dialogue. It's stunning, it's funny, it's downright brilliant.

And it does not belong in your novel. It's got nothing to do with anything, and it sticks out like a sore thumb.

I don't care how much you love it—if it doesn't help make the novel better, *toss that sucker out.* Whimper while you do it, by all means, but ditch it.

Now, take a big drink if you're the drinking type, or have a bar of chocolate. (Or both.) And pat yourself on the back. You've just completed your first Chick Lit novel.

 *Cele-break!*

CONGRATULATIONS!

You've finished your first Chick Lit novel!

THINGS TO DO:

- Get a hot-rock massage. All that typing is enough to put your back and wrists in permanent knots.
- Take a picture of your finished manuscript. Ooooh. That's a lot of pages to be proud of!
- Have a hot fudge sundae. You also burn a lot of calories typing. (At least, that's what I tell myself!)
- Have a "finished manuscript" party with your writing friends. (And, while you're at it, give it to one of them for safekeeping.)

- Soak in a long, hot bath. Envision your book on the *New York Times* Best Seller List.
- Announce your accomplishment on writers' loops (where you know people and are friends with them). The praise will be a nice, soothing balm for the work to come later.
- *Back up your manuscript.* Put it on at least two different backup systems. I burn a CD and then e-mail a copy to myself. If anything bad happens to the computer, or to, say, my house, I know I can find a copy somewhere.
- Buy yourself one special thing. It's a big deal—you deserve it. And if you start associating good things with finishing manuscripts (i.e., every time I finish a manuscript, I get a new pair of shoes) then you'll start training yourself to *want to complete manuscripts.* Which is the whole point!

THINGS *NOT* TO DO:
- Don't start revising immediately.
- Don't ask a family member to read it. (Any family member. Really. Don't do it.)
- Don't start second-guessing yourself or telling yourself that it sucks. You've got no perspective. Just let it rest.
- Don't quit your day job. A finished manuscript is fantastic, but it isn't a sale. And even a sale isn't the best time to quit your day job . . . but we'll talk about that later.

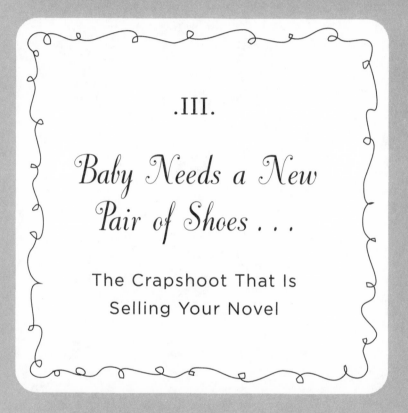

.III.

Baby Needs a New
Pair of Shoes . . .

The Crapshoot That Is
Selling Your Novel

15.

Query Letters, the Chick Lit Way

You've written your first Chick Lit novel. (Or your seventeenth, or whatever.) You've captured a part of your imagination (and your heart) on paper, and now you're setting out on a great new adventure: getting someone in the publishing world to recognize your work for the gem it is, and buy it for a lot of money before giving it a grand launch to reach as many people as possible.

First, a few warnings.

If you think of your book as your baby, you're in for a world of hurt. I'm not saying your book isn't precious. You worked damned hard on that thing, and it's an amazing accomplishment. Having said that, you're going to have to be able to let the book go. If you're scared of sending your "baby" out into the world for fear of what other people say about it, you're never going to get published. It's still precious, and it's still an amazing accomplishment, no matter what anybody—agent or editor or whomever—says about it. But you're going to have to hear a lot of people say, "Man, that's an ugly baby," before you find somebody who falls as much in love with it as you are. Which leads me to the second point . . .

Don't take anything personally. And I mean *anything*. Artists (and writing is definitely an art) are reputed for their sensitivity, and I'm not expecting you to strip your mental gears shifting from gentle creative to barracuda-style businessperson. However, your creative sensitivity has no place on this side of the fence. (It really does help to somehow separate your literary/writing life from your sales life.) You're going to get criticism. More than likely you're going to get very impersonal "no's" from lots of different people. You're probably going to find that at least one person close to you just doesn't get it and harps on you because of your writing. Just keep your head up. Because once you start taking things personally, you'll become a bitter, carping person who only drives success further away. I've seen it, and if you hang around writers' conferences, you'll see it as well—a person who complains incessantly about slights and insults from various editors and agents who are currently milling around. She'll say how mean someone was, how someone else had the temerity to shoot back a form letter rejection without even cracking open her manuscript. She'll alternate between snarling and being near tears. By the end of this person's diatribe, you're convinced that she's going to abandon writing altogether (and maybe move to a Unabomber-style shack out in Montana). But in the next breath, she'll turn to you and say, "And I still don't understand why no one will buy my novel!"

Uh . . . *okay*. Not to be New Age or anything, but what goes around comes around. It takes a lot of energy to be pissed off. It also takes a lot of energy to write. If you've only got a set amount of energy, which would you rather be doing?

Enough said.

Your work is not perfect, nor does it suck. As I've said, once you start to wade into the waters of the publishing world, you're going to get roughed up a bit. Lots of rejections, lots of criticism (constructive and not-so-constructive). Lots of waiting. There are two dangerous reactions to criticism: first, that whoever is criticizing you is crazy, stupid, or worse, because your book is the best thing that's ever landed on his/her desk. Second, that the person is absolutely right, your book is the most dreadful piece of crap ever to be put to paper—it ought to be burned immediately, and you should be slapped soundly for having the gall to send it out in the first place.

Quick! Somebody call the Objectivity Police!

It's tough work. But armed with whatever comfort you need (Häagen-Dazs, say, or your favorite "wooby" blankie), grit your teeth and read any detailed criticism thoroughly. See if you can figure out why they might say what they've said. Is your pacing off, or is there a reason they might think your protagonist is dislikable? Is it something you're willing to change? Is it something you think you might want to change? Or would you rather simply stick with what you've got and send that puppy back out into the world?

The bottom line is: don't make any quick, extreme decisions. Hit a happy medium.

Writing is an art. Selling is a game. And that's what we've moved on to—sales. When you write, unless you're working with a collaborator or you've got an editor asking for a bunch of changes, you're pretty much in complete control of your entire world. You can do whatever you want. It's pure creation.

Selling, on the other hand, depends largely on factors that are outside your control. And you have to take those other factors into consideration when making decisions about the factors that *are* in your control—it's interactive. And there's a way to keep score, handily enough. The minute you sell a novel, you've made a goal. And like any other game, this side of our business can be a lot of fun, if you let it.

Okay, enough lecturing. On to the meat of the matter.

THE QUERY LETTER

You're going to need two important documents before you can start selling your novel. The first is your letter to your target, whether it's an agent or a publisher. We'll go on to picking an agent and a publisher in a minute.

Think of the query letter as an ad. You've got maybe thirty seconds, or possibly only fifteen seconds, to grab your target's attention. That does not mean that you're going to open with a hard sell: "Dear Ms. Agent: This is the greatest novel of all time! BUY NOW!" You're not trying to push cars or meet a quota. Like any good sales item, you're going to need to show that you know your customer, you know your product, and you know why your product is going to be valuable *for your customer.*

You've seen how I go about plotting. Here is my template for how to write the killer query letter.

START WITH YOUR TARGET

The first paragraph of the query letter needs to tell your target, or customer, that you've done your homework. You know who they are, and you're writing to them for a reason. In the case of an agent, you're going to say why you chose them. Maybe someone you know recommended them—and agreed to let you mention them in the letter. That's very important. Mentioning that your critique partner spoke very highly of an agent when querying him/her is subtly suggesting that your critique partner thinks highly enough of *you* to let you bring her up. If your critique partner actually said something like, "Well, my agent is so-and-so, but she's not taking on new clients," then you'll probably feel awful if the agent asks your friend, "So, why did you tell this person to query me?"

Or, maybe you've just done research and discovered that this agent or editor is looking for the type of subgenre you're writing. You'll find out more on how to research agents and editors in later chapters. For now, the important thing is, you'll be writing a short paragraph (a maximum of two or three short sentences) on why you're writing to this person. It can go like this:

Dear Ms. Agent:
I've read several interviews that you've done in various newsletters, and I noticed that you're looking for funny yet dark Chick Lit. I have recently completed a Chick Lit black comedy that I think might interest you. It's called *Just Killing Time* and is 100,000 words in final draft.

That's it. You've shown you know what the target wants. You make the connection: you've just written something that matches what the target wants. Then you give the brief product description: title and word count.

NEXT: THE "SIZZLE"

The next paragraph is where most authors get hung up. You need to encapsulate your novel in a few brief sentences. Like résumés, query letters should not be longer than a page. You're "selling the sizzle, not the steak," to use a very old cliché. You're giving the editor or agent just enough information to intrigue them. You're showing them what the commercial hook is. If you don't know what your commercial hook is, ask yourself: what makes my book different than what's out there currently? What's special about my story? What interests *me* about my story? And then put that in one sentence. Yes, *one*.

It's tough. But if it were easy, everybody would do it.

You could start with a description of your main character. Something that explains why she's interesting, why the reader will either identify with her (such as "Sadie Smith was tired of being stepped on") or be compelled to find out more about her ("Sadie Smith was the most envied 'bitch' in Boston"). Then you drop in your commercial hook: the premise. "Sadie thinks her life is perfect—until she's arrested for insider trading and put under house arrest for a year." Then you put the story goal: "Now, Sadie has to go from high-fashion model to model prisoner, or she'll miss the biggest show of her career." And follow it up with conflict: "The problem

is, how can Sadie get time off for good behavior when she's be-
haved badly all her life?"

Short, direct, and covers the high points. If you're doing an ensemble piece, you'll want the first line to be a quick overview:
"Three friends go back to their high school reunion. . . ." And the
paragraph will be longer, although the descriptions should be short
for each character. "Jamie went from valedictorian to ulcer-ridden
lawyer. Vicki was still, in a manner of speaking, a cheerleader—
acting as the perky sidekick to her successful husband. And Tanya
was still the sulking rebel, although she was finding it harder and
harder to find things to fight for." The premise, story goal, and conflict should be overarching: "The three friends must work together," or, "After twenty years, three women who lost a friendship
after graduation try to regain it in one short weekend."

The biggest temptation here is to try to fit in too many details.
"But it's all important," some authors wail when they see their work
of art crammed into basically the literary equivalent of a shot glass.
Or, "It's misleading—my story isn't like that at all! It's much more
complex, more layered. This makes it sound like something else!"

My agent and editor are probably going to hate me for saying
this, but:

It's not important.

You don't want to completely mislead them, obviously. You
don't want to advertise you've written a "witty romp" when you're
actually doing a literary fiction–type treatise on euthanasia. That's
just mean. But if your story really is about a socialite who goes under house arrest, and it winds up having all these tender moments as
she figures out who she is and why she's so messed up, it's still okay
to emphasize the humor first. Your goal here is not to get across all

the nuances and delicacies of your book. Your goal is to pique inter-est. Your goal is to get a request for a full manuscript. Once they've got the full thing in their hands, *then* they can be impressed by all the details and intricacies. But you're not going to go overboard here.

THE CLOSER

The last paragraph (and there should only be three main paragraphs and a sign-off in this bad boy) is about the other "product" you're selling here: you. I don't mean selling out, and I don't mean anything unsavory. But you're not just selling a book, you're selling a career, and you're advertising that you're a novelist with something to offer. So this last bit tells about why you're qualified to write this story. If you're part of a writer's organization (like Romance Writers of America or the Writers Guild or whatever), include that. If you've won writing contests (recently—not in high school) include that. If you've got any specialized background that qualifies you to write this particular story, definitely write that down. "I worked in high fashion for two years," or "I was under house arrest." (Uh . . . on second thought, maybe you want to leave out that last detail.) But if it's rele-vant, include it. Keep this paragraph to three sentences max, as well.

If you're already published, mention previous titles (only the relevant ones if there are too many to list) along with the publishing houses and pub dates in the closing paragraph. It also helps to en-close clips of good reviews from previous books and/or blurbs for the enclosed manuscript to establish your credibility in the publish-ing world. Prominent newspaper or periodical articles about or written by you will serve to build your reputation with agents and editors, as well.

Lastly, add a sign-off line. "If you enjoy the synopsis, I would be happy to send you the full manuscript of *Just Killing Time*. I have enclosed a self-addressed, stamped envelope for your convenience. Thank you for your time and consideration. I look forward to hearing from you."

That's it. That's your query letter.

It seems easy, but this is something you're going to want to hone down and polish until it's perfect. This one is crucial.

For a full example, see the sample query letters in Appendixes 1 and 2.

16.

You've Got a Voice. Use It!

Synopsis

A lot of people dread writing the synopsis for their book. Writers often feel like they're too short, that they don't really capture what's important in the book. These same people can often write fifty-page essays on their four-hundred page novel, because they're trying to capture the full feel of what their novel stands for. Don't do this. I'm in favor of writing slightly longer synopses, especially if you're writing an ensemble piece, but anything over twenty pages is probably a little nutso.

If you've written your novel using an outline, then writing a synopsis will be a lot easier. For the most part, you'll just be covering the same things you covered when you were building your plot: inciting incident, plot points one through three, black moment, climax, resolution. (And definitely include a resolution. Don't go for a cliff-hanger with the sentence: "If you want to find out what happened, request the full manuscript!" It may sound ridiculous, but people have tried that. Tried, and not succeeded.)

The opening should describe the main character or characters and their most interesting or unique characteristics, as well as plainly state their story goal. Once you've got the goal and the inciting incident sketched out, make sure that the reader can logically follow the action from one paragraph to the next. Ensure that the dramatic sequence and pace comes through clearly. And be very careful that the closing sentence shows that the book's ending will be satisfying. That goes for any synopsis, for any type of commercial novel.

SOME CHICK LIT SYNOPSIS SPECIFICS

The crucial difference between writing a synopsis for any other genre and writing for Chick Lit is this: you're going to want to make sure your synopsis is infused with your writing "voice." (Remember voice? From way back in Chapter 13?)

As I've said, you want to make your story different, but a lot of times, it's hard to invent "something new under the sun" in a subgenre like traditional drinks-and-dating Chick Lit. So what is going to be different is *how* you tell the story—and unless they've got a partial manuscript to go along with the synopsis, which many agents and editors don't want to deal with right off the bat, the best place to showcase your unique voice is in your synopsis.

If you're writing Chick Lit that is funny, make sure there is plenty of humor in the synopsis. Include bits of dialogue if necessary. I know—that seems to go against the purpose of streamlining the synopsis and not including too much information. Don't include whole paragraphs of dialogue. You're going to want to include one or two zingers that actually illustrate a story point.

Using our fictitious Sadie Smith example: Sadie is put under house arrest, but she is assured by hunky policeman Rob Royal that he'll try to keep her life as normal as possible. "I'm used to drinking Cristal in Learjets and rolling in Bentleys with rap stars," she responds acidly. "What were you planning on doing, calling my ankle bracelet 'bling'?"

This illustrates Sadie's sense of humor as well as her past, and the conflict: she's not really cooperating with the police. (It's not a great example, but you get the idea.) Most synopses are written in the third person, present tense. I'm not sure why, but this convention is used even if the book is going to be written in the first person. You could try writing it in the first person, but I think that might be a case of too much voice—it would be overwhelming and make your character possibly seem too self-involved (even if that's not your characterization for her at all). It's not impossible, and it might be worth a try if you think you can pull it off. If you're doing multiple first person, I would suggest not trying it—multiple first person is confusing enough in book-length format. Your own phrasing and descriptions of each character would serve you better.

Another staple of Chick Lit: the background cast of zany secondaries. They might be scene-stealers, but they're also a crucial selling point, so you'll want to make sure that you include descriptions of them. You can do this in paragraph form, but I like to use bullet points, so the reader isn't inundated with character descriptions to keep straight in one very text-dense paragraph. For example:

Now in a new town, with a new job and a new name, Jamie finds herself befriending the patrons of the small bar she works for:

- Carlos, the six-foot-seven albino who "never met a beer he didn't like"
- Therese, the recovering alcoholic and part-time barback
- Genevieve, a flamboyant woman who only comes for weekly karaoke
- Felix, the in-the-closet gay accountant

If you're going to have more than two interesting secondary characters, you'll probably want to make a laundry list of them this way and cover them later. I wouldn't use this approach with main characters, however, since you'll want to go into more detail with them.

I've included a sample synopsis in Appendix 3.

17.

The Great Agent Safari

Finding Representation

D o I really need an agent?"

The short answer is yes. You definitely need an agent if you're going to be serious about having a writing career. Why? Because a good agent can help you come up with a game plan for your writing. He or she will help identify your strengths and suggest how you can capitalize on them; he or she will go to battle for you, become your sales force, and promote you, not only to your publishing house but other publishing houses who might want to work with you down the line. A good agent will be able to negotiate the best possible deal for you. An agent can play bad cop with your publishing house allowing you to remain the good cop (and ensure that your editor will focus on your story when you talk with her, rather than on the the nasty turn negotiations took when you asked for more money on your latest contract).

"So how do I find an agent?"

That's a good question. There are a few questions I think you'll need to answer before you decide what sort of agent you're looking for.

- Where are you in your writing career? Have you sold a book or books before, just not Chick Lit? Have you finished only your first book? Do you know where you want to go with your writing?
- Where do you want your career to go? Seriously, we'd all love to be *New York Times* bestselling authors, and if I had a dime for every time I heard that . . . you get the picture. The real question is, do you see yourself writing one book every year? Every two years? A couple of books a year? Do you want to be in hardcover? Do you want to be able to afford to write full-time? And how much would that take?
- Are you looking for editorial input or not? Do you want an agent who critiques your work, or one who simply sells it?

The answers to all these things will come in very handy once you're shopping for an agent. Shopping for an agent is a lot like looking for a job, actually. The best way to do it is not to go begging, no matter how badly you need it. Instead, focus on the fact that you're a valuable commodity. You're picking them just as much as they're picking you, so you'd better know what you want.

The next old chestnut of advice: *having no agent at all is better than having a bad agent.* Because if you're representing yourself, at least you're with someone you trust. A bad agent will not only prevent you from selling (you could've done that yourself!) but, if you do sell, he or she will botch the deal and claim fifteen percent of your royalties for life. I have heard horror stories of terrible agents who lied to their clients, who never shopped manuscripts, who got low deals and still took their commissions, who got involved with lawsuits. It's a wretched affair, and you don't want to be involved in it. Get a good agent, or don't get one at all.

Having said that, how do you figure out who a good agent is?

DEVELOPING YOUR AGENT LIST

In Chapter 19, I discuss the wealth of on-line resources available for people who want to write Chick Lit. One of those resources is a report called Publisher's Lunch. It comes by e-mail in a weekly report called Lunch Weekly that publicizes book deals that happened that week. While it's not an exhaustive list and it doesn't give exact sales amounts (using euphemisms like "good deal," "nice deal," or "very nice deal" to ballpark what a contract sold for) it's a great way to see what agents are with what authors and what sort of deals they're getting. Karen A. Fox has listings for the women's and romance sections of Lunch Weekly archived on her Web site for at least a year back. The Chick Lit and romance genres are still closely aligned from a business standpoint—the publishers are often the same, as are a lot of the agents. When I was looking for an agent, I went through and catalogued what sort of deals were happening, and I listed all the authors each agent represented, as best I could. This gave me the start of my target list. I wanted to find an agency that was well-reputed, and one that helped develop *New York Times* bestsellers. But not just any bestsellers . . . I wanted ones that represented authors I liked, that I felt had great, quirky, unconventional voices. So I picked my favorite author and found her agency. That was my bull's-eye. Then I created my secondary list from other authors I admired.

RESEARCHING THE LIST

This is going to take some chutzpah on your part, but trust me, it'll be worth it. First, do a Google search on each agent on your list, combined with the word "interview" or "questions" or "article." If that agent has ever been interviewed or quoted in an article or newsletter, you'll be able to see what he or she is like . . . at least, you'll be able to see a little bit of his/her background and philosophy, and get a read on his/her attitude.

Second, you should go to an on-line loop, like Chick Lit Writers, or join the Romance Writers of America's Chick Lit chapter. (It's an on-line chapter—you'll be able to find it in Appendix 7.) After introducing yourself, ask, "Is anyone here represented by or know about" and then name the agent. Say you'd like to query him/her but you wanted to find out more about him/her first. Add, "Private e-mail response is fine," and include your e-mail address. Then thank everyone in advance, and wait. You can also send an e-mail saying, "I write (paranormal Chick Lit, Mommy Lit, whatever). Does anyone have any agents to recommend who are looking for that?" That way, you can also add to your list and cross-reference to see if any agents currently on your list are looking for what you write.

Someone usually e-mails quickly, and you'll be able to get a few responses. Some of it may be rumor or hearsay, comments that start with, "A friend of mine had that agent, and they said he was terrible!" Followed by another e-mail with, "My friend's with that agent, and she thinks he's phenomenal!" So how do you decide who's telling the truth or not?

In that particular case, they might both be, actually. A great agent for one author may be a terrible agent for someone else. Remember those three sets of questions? That's why. Someone who wants no editorial input, who just wants the agent to take what's given to her and sell it, is going to hate an agent who makes suggestions on how to revise proposals and manuscripts. On the other hand, someone who is looking for some editorial feedback because she feels she needs help making her projects more marketable is going to love that same agent.

So, again, how do you figure out who's right for you?

Get information from actual clients or past clients of the agent. Talk to them. In most cases, they'll be happy to answer questions (as long as you're not asking dollar amounts or other nosy contractual questions). When I was searching for my current agent, I looked up three of her current clients and sent them each polite e-mails. I asked the following questions:

- How long have you been with (this agent)?
- What were you looking for when you decided to go with this agent?
- How do you feel this agent does with career strategy?
- How much editorial input does this agent give?
- How do you feel about this agent's negotiation skills?

That first question is important: if you're only asking the questions of new clients who are all in the "honeymoon" phase of the agent/client relationship, you're not going to get as objective a view, and also odds are good the agent hasn't had time to do anything substantial for that client. Try to find a few authors who have been with the agency for several years, if possible. Then, ask questions based on what you want. I knew I wanted to be a bestselling author, but I wanted to keep my artistic integrity, which meant a relatively slow build. I needed someone who had a strength in career strategy, rather than someone who would simply sell what I was giving, no matter how many genres I attempted. I used to hate editorial input from agents, because I believed (and to a certain extent still believe) that it's impossible to serve two masters: if you're going to revise, revise for an editor who's actually buying your book, rather than an agent whose guess is as good as yours is. However, I've since amended my view on this. In this day and age, most editors don't really have time to edit. They are your front line of defense—the ones who fight your battles within the publishing company. They deal with marketing, sales, graphics, scheduling . . . all the other stuff that make or break your novel. They don't have time to help you with craft, at least not as much as they or you would probably like. So a good agent should be able to help pick up the slack to a certain extent—or at least, that's what I was looking for.

Ask current clients your questions, and then add that if they don't feel comfortable answering, you will completely understand. We're not shining a light in anybody's eyes here and grilling them for hours. This is a fact-finding mission.

Come up with your "A-list" of agents. I'd suggest three, although if you've only got one, that's fine, too. You're going to tailor your query letter to show that you did your homework, and then you're going to send off that and your synopsis. And then you're going to wait. You're probably also going to be writing while you wait, which will help take the edge off. Generally, agents answer much more quickly than publishers, which is great.

AGENT HUNTING 101

You'll be getting some rejections—more than likely, form rejections. Again, don't take it personally. This is a very mercurial and very subjective part of the process. Your writing may be brilliant, but the agent just has a "thing" against protagonists like yours . . . because she wears flip-flops, or is a redhead, or whatever. (Yes, unfortunately, it can be that arbitrary.) Or the agent may feel like her agency represents too many authors who are writing something similar to what you're writing, and taking you on would create too much internal competition. Whatever the reason, the bottom line is, they don't have to tell you why, and you shouldn't dwell on it. You've got a list of qualified agents—use it.

With luck (and with a dynamite sales package), you'll get a "nibble"—an agent will be interested in your work. If possible, you will be able to speak with her, either face-to-face at a conference, or at least over the phone. You'll probably feel excited, and it'll be all you can do not to yell, "YES!" into the phone the minute she says, "I'm interested in representing you." Don't jump into anything, however, even if this agent is on the top of your A-list.

SOME QUESTIONS FOR YOUR POTENTIAL AGENT

Tell the agent what sort of career you want to have. Basically, answer the same questions I asked you in the beginning of the chapter. Agents like to know that you've got a plan and goals for your career.

Then, ask your (potential) new agent what she can do to help you achieve those goals. How does he envision your future? What does she like best about your work? What does he think could use improvement? What would she suggest your next step be?

If you want to write hardcover books with quirky heroines dealing with hard-hitting issues and the agent sees you writing mass-market paperbacks that are fluffier with all the emphasis on the humor, then you could be in for a problem, no matter how A-list the agent is. At the same time, if the agent says, "I don't think we have to worry about that right now. You just keep writing books, I'll handle the rest," then I hate to say it, but *run.* You want an agent to handle your negotiations, the business side of things, sure . . . *to a certain extent.* But it's still *your* business. If you just close your eyes and let them handle the rest, I hate to say it, but you're probably going to get screwed. And if you're keeping yourself in the dark, then you're asking for it.

This may seem like a lot of work. It is. But it's worth it, in the long term.

THE AGENCY AGREEMENT

Once you've spoken with the agent and he still wants to represent you, consider whether he's answered your questions satisfactorily. If so, then the next step is making it official—accepting his offer of representation. This usually entails signing an agency agreement. (And if it doesn't, it should.)

Agreements come in different forms, with different language. You will need to read it very carefully. Here are a couple of things to watch out for.

What the agency represents. When I got my agency agreement, the list of everything that the agency represented put the "exhaust" in exhaustive . . . as in, I was exhausted just skimming over it. It didn't just cover novels—it covered any sort of book, screenplay, magazine article, and so on. You name it, they got a cut of it. If somebody paid me for a laundry list, they'd get a percentage. And in case they hadn't thought of it, they made sure to add the phrase "but not limited to" to make sure that it was still covered.

I talked to them. Since they weren't going to help shop things like magazine articles, they agreed to exclude it. I got a few other things excluded, too. The agency is a business, protecting its interests, which I respect. But on the other hand, I don't think anyone is entitled to fifteen percent of my profit without contributing some labor. So if the beautiful day comes when my brilliant women's video game concept comes to fruition and I make a bajillion dollars off of it, I'll keep all of it, since I did all the legwork. Don't be afraid to push back. The worst they can do is say no. If it turns out to be a deal breaker—"Sign all of this, or we won't represent you"—then think long and hard about whether the price is worth it. If you love the agency and are not planning on doing anything but writing novels anyway, go with your instincts and don't make yourself nuts.

"In perpetuity" clauses. These are stipulations that grant that the agency gets fifteen percent of all revenue from a project that they represent, forever—even if you switch agencies at some point down the line, and the new agent gets an even bigger deal on the same book because the rights reverted back to you. They'll still get a fifteen percent cut . . . and so will your new agency. So you'll be losing a total of thirty percent of your revenue.

Some authors are really up in arms about this, and they should be. Remember I was telling you about those horror stories with bad agents? Some bad agents got a project and sat on it, until the author finally left. When the author signed with a new agent who then sold the book—the old agent *still got his cut,* because of the "in perpetuity" clause! Just because he "represented" it—which meant he had it in his desk for six months!

On the other hand, I don't mind the "in perpetuity" clause, if the agency sells the book. If you've chosen your agency wisely and are not looking to jump ship anytime in the near future, that clause is their sign that you're not planning to jump ship—that they should invest their time and energy in you. They should be so stellar that even if you do wind up going to another agency who manages to sell an older property of yours, you wouldn't have expected the first agency to have done anything better. Getting only seventy percent of something you weren't expecting in the first place is better than getting a hundred percent of nothing.

Length of agreement. Here's another bone of contention. Some agencies want a commitment of several years—two, three, or five years, and then you'll go year-to-year after that. This is, again, to see how committed you are to the career, and if it makes it worth their while. Some authors balk at this, thinking it's too constraining. What if things don't work out? What if the agent is terrible? Others find it comforting: you can't ditch them, they can't drop you, no matter what they can't sell. It doesn't really work that way, however. There's generally an escape clause for both parties if it looks like things really, *really* aren't working out. But if you're that afraid, there are agencies that work on a per-project basis. You can always try asking your agent if they'd be open to that sort of arrangement. I'm not a lawyer, and this isn't my bailiwick, but if you've done your homework and talked with the agent, and your instincts say he or she is right—don't worry about the length of agreement. Like most investment plans, you should be thinking about the long term, not necessarily making a killing day trading.

The agent-author relationship is one of the most important in your career. If you're the owner of the company, the agent is going to be your president. (You get to be CEO.) The agent is going to be one of the most important elements on your team. Choose wisely.

18.

It's a Wild World

Approaching Publishers

Some of you may not want to work with an agent, for whatever reason. Some of you might prefer to approach publishers directly. I'd suggest seeing if publishers are open to unagented submissions before going this route, but it's always an option, and there's no law against trying. Even if you want to go with an agent first, which I'd recommend, it's good to know the players—who the big publishers are and what sort of books they're putting out. That helps you work with your agent to find the perfect home for your novel.

WHAT YOU'RE LOOKING FOR

When you're researching publishers, you'll want to look at the following things to see where your novel might find a home.

Who they are already publishing. Avon brings out the offsets of Marian Keyes and the original novels of American Meg Cabot. Pocket puts out books by Jennifer Weiner. Red Dress Ink publishes Sarah Mlynowski and Carole Matthews. NAL/Penguin/Putnam puts out books by Wendy Holden. Kensington has published authors like Stephanie Lehmann. You want to read as much as you can in the genre to see what's already out there—and to find out who you might be similar to, and what sets you apart. If you're writing workplace tell-alls, for example, you might not want to query a publishing house that's already put out three similar stories in the past year.

What they're publishing. Generally, you're going to see a trend within each publishing house, since each will have its own definition of what Chick Lit is (and, consequently, who they're marketing to). If you're writing a frothy and fun traditional Chick Lit, you might not want to target a more literary publisher. Or, if you're trying for a more experimental and slightly darker-toned book, better not to submit to a house that seems to put out only drinks-and-dating-disaster stories.

How many they're publishing a year. You'll need to dig a little deeper to find this information, but the houses that are putting out the most books are usually the publishers that need the most material. This could be a good opportunity for new authors, since the hunger for quality material is greater when there are more spaces to fill.

Here is a nonexhaustive list of publishers and my opinion on what sort of novels they're putting out and what they're looking for. Please note: most of these publishers have their own Web sites. You'll also want to look at secondary sources for more information. These resources are listed in Chapter 19 on on-line networking, as well as Cyberrific Sites to See in Appendix 7.

AVON/HARPERCOLLINS

Avon's Chick Lit imprint is Avon Trade. Avon is a giant in the romance world, and their entry into the Chick Lit world is no less megalithic. Their tone seems to lean more toward the traditional, less toward experimental/dark/literary. If you've got a light tone and a high humor factor, Avon seems like a perfect match. If you're writing Chick Lit for Young Adults (YA), HarperCollins has their immensely successful HarperTorch imprint. This runs the gamut from light, fun stories to mysteries, paranormal, and deeper, more emotional reads.

BALLANTINE/IVY

A division of Random House. They have published books like *Miss Match* by Leslie Carroll and *Beginner's Luck* by Laura Pedersen. They also publish paranormal Chick Lit, namely Shanna Swendson's Enchanted, Inc. series. One of their hardcover Lady Lit titles is *The Goddesses of Kitchen Avenue* by Barbara Samuel. They seem to have eclectic tastes.

BANTAM/DELL

The publishers of the Shopaholic series and books like Sue Margolis's *Apocalipstick*, they publish fun books and, in the case of Sue

Margolis, books with more of an edge. They explore less romantic comedy and more ethnic and family drama in *Hostile Makeover* by Wendy Wax. If your Chick Lit hovers on the edge of women's fiction as far as dramatic content but still retains a sharply comedic edge, this could be a good house to target.

BERKLEY

More recently breaking into the Chick Lit market, Berkley is an imprint of the Penguin/Putnam conglomerate. See listing under NAL for its sister imprints in Chick Lit. They are also coming out with a YA line in coordination with NAL/Penguin/Putnam. The imprint is called Jam.

DORCHESTER

A smaller, independent publisher, they were relative latecomers to the Chick Lit game. Their introduction to the genre: *American Idle* by Alesia Holliday. Dorchester tends toward the more traditional but is also known for taking risks. One of their most successful Chick Lit–voiced authors is Katie MacAlister. They have a YA imprint called Smooch, featuring very Chick Lit–voiced books. Katie MacAlister's alter ego, Katie Maxwell, is one of their featured authors in the Smooch line, with books like *The Year My Life Went Down the Loo*.

KENSINGTON

Built up primarily from their romance genre business, Kensington introduced the Strapless line, featuring the now-stereotypical candy-colored covers and cute illustrations or graphics. They tend more toward traditional Chick Lit, Mommy Lit, and things geared toward a slightly younger demographic (thirties and younger). Some example titles: *Are You in the Mood?* by Stephanie Lehmann, *Ex-Girlfriends* by Kylie Adams, and *Reinventing Mona* by Jennifer Coburn.

NAL

Part of the Penguin/Putnam/Berkley conglomerate, they put out trade-sized Chick Lit, such as Liz Maverick's *Adventures of an Ice Princess*. They are also developing several Chick Lit mystery series, and publish the Bubbles Unbound mystery series previously mentioned.

POCKET BOOKS

With their Downtown Press imprint for Chick Lit, Pocket Books has a slightly more literary and serious tone. For the truly literary women's fiction, they have their Atria imprint. They have authors such as Lisa Tucker and Sister Souljah. Their parent company, Simon and Schuster, also has YA offerings under the imprint Simon Pulse, but these don't seem very Chick Lit–friendly.

RED DRESS INK

Publishing two titles a month (as of this printing), Red Dress Ink publishes the gamut of Chick Lit, conquering by sheer number. They have traditional Chick Lit, mystery, literary, and Matron/Hen Lit. They publish in trade size and hardcover, with occasional mass-market paperback rereleases. They also have a long response time—be patient.

STEEPLE HILL CAFÉ

Another imprint from the Harlequin conglomerate, this is for Christian Chick Lit only. Some of their titles include *Love the Sinner* by Lynn Bulock and *Sadie-in-Waiting* by Annie Jones.

ST. MARTIN'S PRESS

St. Martin's has been groundbreaking when it comes to Chick Lit: they are the publishers for Jennifer Crusie's women's fiction, as well as Janet Evanovich's Stephanie Plum mystery series. They also published Emma McLaughlin and Nicola Kraus's bestselling *The Nanny Diaries* and Adèle Lang's *Confessions of a Sociopathic Social Climber*. St. Martin's also publishes Thomas Dunne Books, a separate imprint—*Confessions* was published under this imprint, as was Jill Smolinski's *Flip-Flopped*, and Jennifer Manske Fenske's *Toss the Bride*. If you want to create a new subgenre, this is a good place to go for it.

WARNER

With their relatively new imprint 5 Spot, Warner is diving into the Chick Lit fray with "hip entertainment" in both fiction and nonfiction formats. In press releases and publicity, they are quoted as saying they are marketing to "chicks with brains" and their books will be about more than women who need a new boyfriend and a new pair of Manolos. If you're writing traditional Chick Lit, you'll probably want to steer clear. If you're writing something dark, this could be your new home. Their launch titles included *Princess Izzy and the E Street Shuffle* by Beverly Bartlett.

L ook up each on-line for guidelines and new offerings. The more you know about the publishing industry, the easier it is to "play the game" of getting your novel published.

Think of it as fantasy football for women's fiction writers. It's more fun when you know all the teams.

19.

Welcome to the Matrix

On-line Networking

S ome of my best friends are people I've never met.

That may sound strange, but with the advent of the Internet, I've made friends with writers from around the country—and around the world, for that matter. They say that writing is a solitary profession, and they're not wrong. It's tough to stay cooped up all day, typing words that may or may not ever see the light of day, having no coworkers to kibbutz with about what you're working on. (That's not to say you might not have coworkers. I wrote my first five novels while working at a day job of one sort or another. Still, kibitzing with day job workers is different than socializing with other writers.) When you're in the process of writing, networking with other writers can be fantastic. They can help you with brainstorming if you're stuck, or they can simply be sympathetic shoulders to cry on when you've hit a writer's block the size of Toledo. At the same time, there's nothing quite so inspiring as being able to give advice to someone else who's stuck, or to a new writer who knows even less about the craft and business of writing than you did when you started out. Networking is a way of keeping your creative lymphatic system circulating. If you stay in your own personal vacuum for too long, you'll find yourself getting both stale and discouraged.

WHERE EVERYBODY KNOWS YOUR NAME (OR YOU KNOW THEIRS)

There are a couple of places on-line where you can participate in discussions or simply read discussions that are going on. The first and most legendary Yahoo! Group for people who like to write Chick Lit is Deanna Carlyle's Chick Lit Loop. You can subscribe by writing an e-mail to "chicklit-subscribe@yahoogroups.com" (For more information on this loop, or list-serv, check out Deanna's site at www.deannacarlyle.com/chick-lit.html). Started in 2001, this loop is approximately one thousand members strong, and the numbers are growing every day. After you join, you can post a quick e-mail introducing yourself, or you can "lurk," which means reading what everyone else is posting without putting yourself in the public eye at all. You might want to do this a while if you feel self-conscious. If you've got questions or really need some feedback/friendship/whatever right off the bat, an introduction is the way to go. Keep it brief and to the point: "Hi, I'm (your name). I am interested in writing (kind of Chick Lit, if you know), and I look forward to hearing what you've got to say. Thanks!" You'll get a wave of welcomes. As a member, you'll be able to read in the archives what people have talked about previously.

Another great group is Chick Lit Writers of the World, an international chapter of the Romance Writers of America. It is approximately three hundred members strong and they're largely on-line. Their Web site address is www.chicklitwriters.com. To become a member, you need to join both the RWA (membership runs about $70 for the year) and the chapter itself (chapter membership is about $25 for the year). They have tremendous resources: interviews and chats with editors and agents are archived, and many members published in Chick Lit who are happy to answer questions. It's a great environment. They also have an e-mail loop if you're not feeling social on-line.

There is one thing to be careful of: posts from these two groups can be voluminous. You could go from getting maybe thirty e-mails a day to three hundred in an afternoon—and no, that's not an exaggeration. You might want to consider going on digest, which bundles about twenty-five e-mails into one long post. That way, you can scan the subject headers inside the e-mail and decide which topics you're interested in reading about. Otherwise, once you join Yahoo! Groups, you can simply opt to view the forum on-line, in the Yahoo! Group itself, rather than have it send anything to e-mail. That way, you can do searches, look at subject lines, and simply get what you want rather than wade through every single e-mail. That's less social, but if you're looking specifically for information, it might be more productive.

For those writers who are trying to get published, on-line groups can provide a wealth of information. I've often joked that when a senior editor for a Chick Lit publisher drops her pencil, somebody on-line knows fifteen minutes later. Which means that all the rest of us know in approximately one hour. By keeping my ear to the ground, electronically speaking, I found out about new publisher projects and imprints faster than my old agent did. It's hard for agents to keep their fingers on every single pulse out there, especially if he or she is representing more than simply the Chick Lit or women's fiction realm. You need to find out information on your own, rather than simply rely on your agent to tell you what's happening in the world around you.

You can also find out information on agents and editors themselves. Whether you correspond with published authors or just glean information from interactions fellow unpublished writers have had with these professionals, you'll be able to get secondhand facts before you go on your publishing quest. For example, you'll find out that one particular editor is always backlogged—he's got at least six months' worth of manuscripts on his desk, and he doesn't even get back to his own authors in a timely fashion, much less prospective writers. You might even find out about a new imprint and a brand-new editor who just happens to be in the market for ethnic literary Chick Lit for "mixed race" readers—exactly what you're writing.

A note of caution: be wary of negative information that you receive. If you ask for "the dirt" from published authors, you will probably be considered unprofessional. Most authors are wary of their professional relationships and don't want to burn bridges, even if their last agent or editor was, shall we say, less than ideal. So some authors will be hesitant to tell you anything about their prior professional associates. On the other hand, some authors will be more than willing to give you a full hatchet job on their "ex," be it agent or editor. You'll want to take these with a grain of salt as well. For one thing, for every author that hates an agent or an editor, you'll find another author that raves about the exact same agent/editor. For another, you're only getting one side of the story. Authors who are bitter may speak too harshly, without thinking of anything besides getting your support and sympathy. Listen to as many sides as you can—and don't jump to any conclusions rashly. Go with your instincts. And, if necessary, you can see if an agent has had any claims filed against him/her. If the agent is listed with the Association of Authors' Representatives then they should be all right.

In Appendix 7, I've got a list of other cool and fun Web sites for anybody who wants to write Chick Lit. This includes publisher information, Chick Lit review sites, and some miscellaneous sites like Wordspy, which, if nothing else, will kill time when you're trying to procrastinate!

20.

Girls' Night In

How to Form a Crit Group

One thing that I tell all authors who are serious about becoming writers: at some point, you'll want to join a critique group, especially if you're just starting out and feeling a little hesitant. "Crit groups" are groups of writers, usually no fewer than three and no more than six. They meet on a regular basis, exchange writing samples, and provide feedback on one another's work.

When I initially started writing, I joined my first critique group with a lot of trepidation. I'd never let anyone read my work, other than some little things in high school. It was enough to make me nauseous. But I met usually once a month with three other women writers. I'd make copies of one chapter for everyone, and we'd spend the first half hour or so reading one another's photocopies.

It helped that all of the women were also very new (and very scared). The critique group would turn into a mass brainstorming session. An old friend of mine used to call this "in my version of your book." Each critique partner would say, "That was really good!" and then suggest something that she'd like to see: she'd like the scene to end happily, instead of on such a downer; she'd like to see the heroine as a brunette instead of a blonde; she'd like to see it as more of a murder mystery (since, coincidentally, the story she was working on was a mystery). After about nine meetings, I left the group. It had been a great, supportive, and fun experience, and if nothing else, it inspired me to keep writing because I felt guilty and lazy when I didn't bring anything to the table. However, I knew that I needed to find another group that, to use a grossly overused expression, "kicked it up a notch."

My next group met every single Monday night for three hours. It was, needless to say, a different vibe altogether. There were still four of us, again, and all women. (Later, we added a fifth, a man whose insight often had me howling with laughter, even if I was simultaneously stinging with pain at the sharpness of the comment.) We each brought shorter amounts, generally a scene. And the resultant conversations tended to hover somewhere between a spirited debate on *Frontline* and blood sport at the Colosseum. We were ruthless. I also learned more, and became more accomplished, with that critique group than I ever would have on my own. I wrote my first two novels while meeting with them, once a week, rain or shine.

The thing is, I could not have jumped into that second critique group right off the bat. As nervous as I was about having other people read (and, God forbid, *judge*) my writing, I would've run screaming after the first meeting and never written another word. I had to gauge my own comfort level. I had to build up.

I would suggest that you join a group or form your own. If you're wondering how, you might consider joining the Romance

Writers of America. Now, before you're scared off by the whole "Romance" aspect of the name, don't worry—it's not all Fabio and soft-core porn. The RWA is an amazing organization, with local chapters that meet in every state in the country, not to mention countless on-line chapters (like the Chick Lit chapter). You could go to a chapter meeting, and then stand up during the announcements section and introduce yourself. Say that you write Chick Lit and that you're looking to join a critique group. Of course, the established critique groups may be romance-only, but more and more writers are turning to Chick Lit because it has a more fun and relevant voice, it has a lot fewer constraints than the romance genre generally has, and it pays a lot more for newer authors, or at least, it has historically. At any rate, if on-line networking isn't filling your social needs as well as face-to-face time, this might be an outlet to look into. Personally, I've been to chapter meetings all over the West Coast, and I've been to RWA-sponsored conferences all over the country. You could not meet a nicer group of women, period. And the amount of information they're willing to share is mind-blowing. You can find a local chapter by going to www.rwanational.org and clicking on "Chapters." They'll give you a map and a list of chapters by state. Almost every chapter has its own Web site with dates and times for local meetings. If you've already joined the RWA and the Chick Lit Writers of the World chapter, then you might post a message saying, "I'm in (location), and I'm looking for any authors nearby who want to start a critique group."

If all else fails, you can always post a flyer at your local library or coffee shop, saying that you write women's fiction and Chick Lit and you're looking to start a writing group. You could also try on-line groups, like Meetup.com or Craigslist.com, and post the same information in a virtual flyer. Pick a date, and see who shows up.

GOOD FENCES MAKE GOOD CRIT PARTNERS: SOME BASIC RULES

To have a successful group, it's best to keep the number relatively low. You'll also want to make sure that every single person is "on the same page," so to speak, as far as the goals of the critique group. Ask the following of each member:

Where are you in your writing? With any luck, you'll be fairly close in experience and skill levels. You wouldn't necessarily want one person to have written eighteen novels, and another one just finishing her first chapter of her first book *ever*. Those kind of inequities create problems, since the person with tons of books probably doesn't want to act as a teacher, and the one writing her first book might feel bad that she doesn't know enough to comment in an educated fashion. Find out where everybody stands.

What are you writing? You don't necessarily all need to be writing the same thing—if you're all writing traditional Chick Lit, you might feel a little competitive (or intimidated), or worse, you might all start to sound similar to one another because you're so familiar with one another's work. On the other hand, if one of you is writing Tart Noir–style Chick Lit and another is writing Christian Chick Lit, and each hates the other's subgenre, you could be in for some problems. Make sure there are no hot buttons or things that people "absolutely hate" that would taint their readings and feedback.

What do you want out of this critique group? This is the biggie, and honestly, no matter what someone says, you'll find out the truth a few weeks in, through how each person acts. (Which is why it's important to set up a trial period. More on that in a minute.) The important thing to establish is whether people want to brainstorm, or hate brainstorming; if they're looking for constructive criticism; if they know where their weak points are, or if they're trying to figure that out. Because if one person goes in expecting to hear other people's ideas on how to make her book better and another goes in with the intention of giving the roughest critique possible to try to help that person grow, you're going to wind up with two very unhappy people by the end of the night. The first person will be in tears because she got ripped to shreds, and the second person will tear her hair out because she just got a bunch of wimpy compliments and alternate ideas that she had no interest in (instead of some tangible critiques that would improve her writing). Most people don't realize how vulnerable it makes you when you put your heart and writing on the block and declare it open season.

Once you've got these questions answered, you'll want to set a few ground rules. The first is how often you meet and where. Maybe you can rotate, especially if group members are coming from far away—that way, you don't have one poor soul commuting a great distance each time while the other is just popping down to her local Starbucks. On the other hand, you don't necessarily want to impose on the hospitality of one member, either, unless she really doesn't mind a group of writers descending en masse in her living room every two weeks. Which brings up my next point: I would suggest meeting every two weeks, if not every week, if possible. If you meet once a month, you are tempted to procrastinate. You think, "I still have time to write that chapter," and then you're scrambling the day before it's due. Or, you don't write . . . and then you feel guilty and skip the meeting. That's no good. Meeting weekly really holds your feet to the fire—but with today's hectic schedules, it isn't always realistic. Biweekly is your best bet.

The next ground rule: trial period. Critique groups aren't machines—they're comprised of writers with very different personalities, and no matter how good your intentions are, not all personalities will get along. It can take a while for a good critique group to gel, and often different people will rotate in and out of the group. State that at the outset. Say you'll have four to six meetings to decide how the group's going—after that, anyone can leave at will. (Not that they can't leave before that, but the idea is that everybody knows it's a test and hopefully there will be no hard feelings. This gives an out clause to those who need it.) If someone who you don't like chooses to stay, even if you like everybody else, you should opt out. You can maybe partner with one or two of the others on a separate basis for feedback, or form a separate critique group with them later.

The third ground rule: this is trickier, but you might want to include a "tempering" procedure. All critiques should include one positive thing, even if it's, "You typed this really well." (I wouldn't recommend that, by the way, but it's a start.) That way, nobody feels completely hammered or hated by the other members. It may not be necessary, especially if everyone has written several manuscripts and has regularly faced the perils and harsh rejections of editors and agents. However, if somebody's a little *too* gleeful about ripping other manuscripts to shreds, it might help rein her in a little.

Finally, be careful about getting stuck on your critique group's criticisms. Critique groups can be very valuable and helpful tools for your writing, as well as a way to develop some great friendships. However, if you find yourself fixing your writing simply to please your critique group—or if you find that you're working on the same scene, over and over, with no seeming improvement—gently thank them and move on. Critique groups should be primarily about one thing: *helping you get published.* Anything else is a social activity.

CONGRATULATIONS!

You've just sold your first Chick Lit novel!

THINGS TO DO:

- Tell every single person you know. Your mailman, your alumni club, that weird guy at the grocery store who seems to know your name. Tell them you're going to remind them again when the book hits shelves.
- Have a really decadent night out on the town.
- Breathe. (It's amazing how you might forget to do that once you get The Call from an editor saying she wants to buy your manuscript.)
- Buy a really cute outfit . . . one you can see yourself signing books in.
- Start planning your promotion. Talk to friends and other published authors about some basics.
- Start planning your next novels—and *turn in proposals.* You're not a success with just one book. It's every other book that makes your career.

- E-mail me at cathy@cathyyardley.com, and let me know what your book is and when it's coming out. I'd love to hear about it!

THINGS TO NOT DO:

- Blow your entire advance on a new wardrobe. You can blow it on promotion, or a new computer, or stuff like that, because you can deduct it (consult your accountant first). But limit your spending to, say, half your advance.
- Don't quit your day job, unless you've got a spouse who is willing to be a "patron of the arts." Donald Maass recommends that you keep another source of income until you've got five books that remain in print generating royalties. It's a good benchmark.

Congratulations!

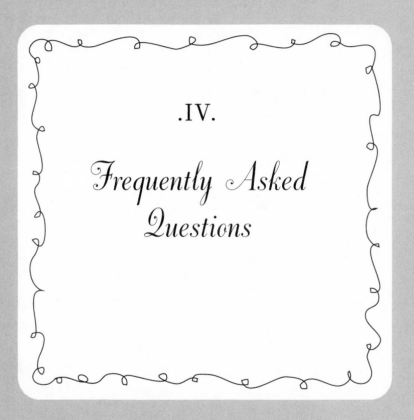

.IV.

Frequently Asked Questions

21.

Questions I'm Asked All the Time

As a published author, I travel around a lot, promoting my books and speaking to various writing organizations about how to write Chick Lit and other writing-related topics. Invariably, I am asked some of the same questions over and over, from San Diego to Seattle to Boston. So I thought I'd share some of them with you, with the answers I usually give, in case you had some of the same issues on your mind.

I'M NOT COOL ENOUGH/YOUNG ENOUGH/ HIP ENOUGH/FUNNY ENOUGH TO WRITE CHICK LIT, AM I?

Yes, you are.

Despite how it appears based on the early Chick Lit novels and the traditional Chick Lit novels that are coming out, you don't need to be a twentysomething fashionista who is so cool and so hip that you sleep in your Prada sunglasses. Chick Lit is more about having a certain attitude about life than about being trendy and popular. You can have a Chick Lit attitude at any age. Chick Lit does require a certain sense of humor and the ability to not take yourself—or pretty much anything else—too seriously. It's about resilience, about the ability to bounce back even if you whine and indulge in retail therapy before you do. It's not about characters who are perfect, who are martyrs, or who are Stepford Wives (although if you're writing a character like Bree from *Desperate Housewives,* then it's completely appropriate). Chick Lit isn't limiting. And don't worry about not being funny enough, unless you're writing a tragedy. The ending should be upbeat, granted. But you can still tackle "meaty" subject matter, like death, divorce, and other upheavals. Just have confidence.

DO I HAVE TO WRITE IN THE FIRST PERSON? MOST OF THE BOOKS I'VE READ ARE IN THE FIRST PERSON, BUT I DON'T LIKE WRITING THAT WAY.

You don't have to write in the first person.

I was giving a talk at the Romance Writers of America national convention on what Chick Lit is and how to write it. A woman asked this question specifically. I answered that when I wrote *L.A. Woman*, it was the sixth book that Red Dress Ink published, and it was their first that wasn't written in the first person. Instead, it was written in the third person, from three different character viewpoints. She frowned and said, "Well, of course *you* could. You're this big author. You can break the rules."

I immediately started laughing. *L.A. Woman* was my first Chick Lit novel, and I still broke the rules. To this day, I have no idea what "big author" she thought I was!

Again, it comes down to confidence, and what you think the story needs. Don't feel constrained by what other people are doing.

WHAT ARE THE RULES FOR WRITING CHICK LIT?

Do you remember that comic strip *Calvin and Hobbes*? They played a game called Calvinball where there weren't any set rules. I think the only rule was you couldn't have the same rule twice.

You may be wondering why I'm referencing this.

Chick Lit, and pretty much all of publishing, plays a lot like Calvinball. There aren't any rules. (Or if there are, nobody's told me. If you get a copy, please e-mail me!) What's more, lots of people who don't know might tell you that there are rules. "You can't write that. I've read lots of Chick Lit, and there's not enough sex, or too much sex, or not enough pop culture references." They'll sound utterly knowledgeable when they tell you this. But they're wrong. Just go with your gut.

CAN MY CHARACTERS SWEAR?

Hell, yes! (Sorry. That was too easy.) They can swear. There are no language police, and you want your characters to be real, three-dimensional, and modern. There is a lot of swearing in modern usage, even by (and in some cases especially by) women. It's just a matter of appropriateness. (If you've got a fifty-seven-year-old society matron having tea at her favorite country club, don't have her ask to "pass the fucking sugar," unless it's done for deliberate comedic effect.)

DO MY CHARACTERS HAVE TO SWEAR?

Absolutely not. Especially if you're writing for something like Christian Chick Lit. Besides, swearing is like any other seasoning—add too much, and that's all people are going to notice. In fact, it's sometimes better to throw readers for a loop. If you've got a character working in an environment where swearing is prevalent—say, your protagonist is a woman working in a construction crew—have her boss be someone who refuses to swear, even though he looks like the type. It's those kinds of contradictions that make strong characters.

Never feel like you "have" to do anything that goes against your grain simply because you've been told it's a genre convention. That's how the genre evolves.

I'M WRITING A BOOK ABOUT (WHATEVER). IS THIS STILL CHICK LIT? HOW CAN I TELL?

You can tell if your book is still Chick Lit by how you think it would be marketed. Do you have a humorous take on the subject? (Not necessarily laugh-out-loud funny, but at the very least a quirky viewpoint?) Is it a women's fiction story . . . that is, does it pertain to women's interests? Do you see it as a commercial genre fiction novel or literary fiction? (If you don't know the difference, don't feel bad. Most people don't, and there's no easy definition for either.)

The thing is, if you've got a story that's a coming-of-age or coming-of-consciousness story, that has even a modicum of humor, like it or not, odds are good a publisher would call it Chick Lit anyway, whether you want it to be or not. These days, any contemporary women's fiction written by female novelists between the ages of twenty to forty is getting slapped with the label of "Chick Lit" because it's a genre that sells enormously well, or at least has historically. Zadie Smith, a brilliant young novelist from England shortlisted for the Booker Prize, published her breakout novel *White Teeth* . . . and promptly got lumped with the proliferation of Chick Lit authors who wrote in England, even though she didn't consider her novel to be Chick Lit at all.

So don't worry. If your story is told from women's viewpoints, odds are good it's Chick Lit. If you're really stressed out about it, ask an agent or your writing friends who are familiar with Chick Lit. They'll tell you.

I READ THAT THE CHICK LIT TREND IS OVER. SHOULD I EVEN BOTHER WRITING ONE?

People who say that the Chick Lit trend is over don't understand what the genre really is. Chick Lit is a different way of viewing women. (Forgive me while I pull out a soapbox here.) Back in the day, women's fiction was populated with either glitzy super-bitches à la *Dynasty* or ideal martyrs dealing with hardship after heartbreak, à la Danielle Steel novels. With Chick Lit, you saw women who were still dealing with hardship, but they weren't "perfect" about it. They broke down, they cursed, they drank, they hung out with their friends and commiserated. And then they picked up the pieces and—with some hard work, humor, and an unsinkable attitude—they wound up on top.

And a lot of readers picked up these books and thought: *these women are a lot like me*. And consequently read a lot more of them.

Chick Lit is a recognition of today's woman. You see a reflection of the changing roles of women in culture. The issues that Chick Lit addresses are relevant to any woman in today's society: the fact that the age that most people get married is going up; the fact that more women are in upwardly mobile careers and are buying their own houses; the fact that gender roles are changing; and the fact that women *still* want to get married and have kids, and face their own challenges around that. In addition, Chick Lit often reflects a change in societal structure. Today, most women's "families" are built around a knot of friends, while their blood families are the source of both love and great tension (elements also covered in Chick Lit novels).

I can't say if "Chick Lit" will continue as a marketing moniker. But relevant women's stories are always going to thrive, no matter what genre name they're sold under. Why?

Because women read.

EVERYBODY CALLS CHICK LIT DUMB, ANTIFEMINIST, AND A BUNCH OF OTHER BAD THINGS. WHAT DO YOU THINK?

The short and diplomatic answer: I disagree entirely.

The long and mean answer: Those people need to get a life and get a sense of humor transplant, stat. Jeez!

Chick Lit is not the end of Western Civilization as we know it. It's not dumb, or at least, it doesn't have to be. It's certainly not antifeminist. Since when has wanting to fall in love been antifeminist? Since when has carping about an evil boss set the women's movement back a hundred years? Okay, there is some Chick Lit out there that revolves around finding a rich husband, but those are usually twisted to show the protagonist figuring out that a sugar daddy might not be the best plan. So it's not even espousing that sort of view. If anything, Chick Lit doesn't pretend that women are any worse or any more virtuous than real women are.

Having said that, most Chick Lit reviews are labeled "frothy," "lightweight," and "frivolous." If you're going to have a problem with those sort of labels being slapped on your work, you're in the wrong line of business. You know what your book is. What's more important is knowing who your audience is. Your readers are not dumb. The minute you think they are, you're going to start sabotaging your book, subconsciously and fatally. You need to respect your readers, your book, and yourself.

Most of all, if you have fun with it, then you're doing the right thing. You've had a whole lifetime of doing unpleasant stuff because you felt you had to. Going to the gym. Going to a day job. Eating lima beans is a prime example.

Write what you enjoy, and odds are good that other people will enjoy reading it, too.

Yes. It really can be that simple.

PARTING SHOT: RELEASE YOUR INNER CHICK

I've said it a million times, and I'll say it again: Chick Lit is more than a genre, it's an attitude. One that portrays contemporary women in a truthful but not harsh light. One that embraces both our silly flaws and our best qualities. Is that to say that every woman is a shallow and superficial ditz with a Kate Spade purse full of credit cards, worried about finding Mr. Right before her biological clock stops? No, of course not. But even as an educated, articulate, and (I'd like to think) intelligent modern woman, I know that I've found comfort on the wrong side of retail therapy instead of curling up with some Nietzsche. Just because I bought a pair of Steve Madden slides doesn't mean I suddenly disregard environmental issues. And as far as finding Mr. Right and worrying about one's biological clock—I know that finding a husband/boyfriend/life partner isn't going to bring about world peace. I'm even secure enough to know that I don't need a man in my life to have . . . well, a life, and I mean that in the most complete way possible. However, I also know that at eleven thirty on Valentine's Day, all the platitudes in the world aren't going to stand between me and a box of dark chocolate truffles if I'm single and feeling lonely. Compound that with the very real thought that after a certain age, having kids is difficult—if not impossible—and remind me again why I shouldn't consider the issue important?

One of the sharpest (and most famous) detractors of the Chick Lit genre is the British author Doris Lessing, who said: "It would be better, perhaps, if [Chick Lit writers] would write about their lives as they really saw them, and not these helpless girls, drunken, worrying about their weight and so on."

When I was in college, sophomore year, I was assigned a novel in one of my sociology classes. It was about a woman who wrote in not one diary, but four . . . compartmentalizing her life in each, one for her relationships, one for her political activism, one for her career, etc. She finally combined them all into one journal at the end, showing her embrace of all sides into one integrated woman. I read it in the study lounge for hours. I devoured it. And the thing that struck me the hardest were her descriptions of her relationships. How could a female protagonist so obviously intelligent, thoughtful, involved in such huge sociopolitical causes, still be jerked around by these men? How could this heroine sacrifice so much of herself to keep them happy? Why would she? It was fascinating. When I started writing Chick Lit, I remembered that novel, and her, as the prototype—the first book that really captured the emotion that Chick Lit should cover. A balancing act, a coming-of-consciousness, a way to become whole by recognizing the dumb things we do and still accepting them.

That novel was *The Golden Notebook* by Doris Lessing. And, to me, it's one of the finest examples of Chick Lit out there. (And won't she just be thrilled to hear that one?)

To address her statement: strangely enough, I have been (on occasion) drunk. I've been five to thirty-five pounds too heavy. And, in several dark and somber circumstances, I have felt absolutely helpless.

Exactly how would she think that this isn't writing about my real life?

Chick Lit doesn't have to be light. It doesn't have to be serious. It doesn't *have* to be *anything*. Chick Lit is simply this: stories about contemporary women, for contemporary women.

So if you want to tackle issues like alcoholism and drug abuse and abortion and racial tension, and you want to illustrate it by showing real women dealing with them with grace, humor, and a whole lot of attitude—go for it!

And if you just want to write something fun so real women who are dealing with those issues have something to read to blow off steam—go for it!

The important thing? Make sure it's *your* book. Push the boundaries of Chick Lit as far as they'll go. Take chances. Write your biggest dreams, your dirtiest secrets, your nastiest fears. Write things so honest, they scare the hell out of you. Write things that would cause your parents to wonder what the neighbors might think. Hell . . . shock the neighbors.

Don't worry about what any other person on earth has to say about it. We might not be finding the cure to cancer, but fun or not, our books have the power to change people's lives. Even if it's only our own.

That's cause enough for me. Every book I write makes me more of a protagonist in my own life. Drop me a line at cathy@cathy yardley.com, and let me know how your book changes yours.

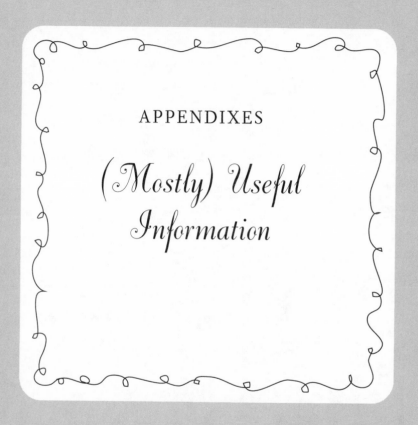

APPENDIXES

(Mostly) Useful Information

APPENDIX 1

Sample Query Letter—Agent

Ms. Elizabeth Agent
Bigshot Literary Agency
1111 Big Street, Suite Z
New York, NY 11111

Dear Ms. Agent:

I recently read the transcript of an interview you had with the Chick Lit Books Web site and noticed that you were very interested in ethnic Chick Lit, as well as mother-daughter stories. Several of your clients are friends of mine, and Suzy Somebody suggested that I query you. I have an Asian American story involving a mother and a daughter that might suit your interests. Titled *None of the Above*, it is 100,000 words in final draft.

Janice Nagle flies from her artist's loft in Berkeley back to her parents' home in upstate New York when her grandmother dies . . . only to discover that her father has been carrying on an affair and, with Grandma's death, plans to divorce Janice's mother, Mai. Mai and Janice have never really gotten along, since Mai is the embodiment of old-world, Asian conservative, and Janice, at age twenty-nine, seems to still have some rebellion issues. So when Janice is maneuvered into letting her mother move all the way across the country to move in with her, it's a cross-cultural disaster waiting to happen. In the course of the story, Janice learns more about the mother who always seemed more like a warden, and Mai learns how to be more like the woman she was before she lost herself in marriage. In the end, they both learn how to accept each other for the women that they've become.

I am half Asian and half American, and this story is close to my heart, since I have not seen many Chick Lit books that deal with mixed ethnicities. I have been writing for the past five years. I have won the Silver Birch Award for writing excellence and I've been a member in good standing of the Romance Writers of America since 2002.

Enclosed please find the synopsis for *None of the Above* and a self-addressed, stamped envelope. I would be happy to send the full manuscript at your request. Thank you for your time and consideration. I look forward to hearing from you.

Sincerely,

Annie Writer

APPENDIX 2

Sample Query Letter—Editor

Ms. Rachel Editor
Chick Lit Publishing House
1111 Big Street, Suite Z
New York, NY 11111

Dear Ms. Editor:

In the latest issue of Publisher's Lunch, I read that Chick Lit Publishing House was looking for material for a new ethnic imprint. I have just finished a manuscript that I think fits your needs. Titled *None of the Above*, it is 100,000 words in final draft.

Janice Nagle flies from her artist's loft in Berkeley back to her parents' home in upstate New York when her grandmother dies . . . only to discover that her father has been carrying on an affair and, with Grandma's death, plans to divorce Janice's mother, Mai. Mai and Janice have never really gotten along, since Mai is the embodiment of old-world, Asian conservative, and Janice, at age twenty-nine, seems to still have some rebellion issues. So when Janice is maneuvered into letting her mother move all the way across the country to move in with her, it's a cross-cultural disaster waiting to happen. In the course of the story, Janice learns more about the mother who always seemed more like a warden, and Mai learns how to be more like the woman she was before she lost herself in marriage. In the end, they both learn how to accept each other for the women that they've become.

I am half Asian and half American, and this story is close to my heart, since I have not seen many Chick Lit books that deal with mixed ethnicities. I have been writing for the past five years. I have won the Silver Birch Award for writing excellence and I've been a member in good standing of the Romance Writers of America since 2002.

Enclosed please find the synopsis for *None of the Above* and a self-addressed, stamped envelope. I would be happy to send the full manuscript at your request. Thank you for your time and consideration. I look forward to hearing from you.

Sincerely,

Annie Writer

APPENDIX 3

Sample Synopsis

None of the Above
CHICK LIT NOVEL
Approximately 100k words

Janice Nagle grabs the first flight back to upstate New York when she gets the call that her grandmother has died. It's not a huge surprise—her grandmother was eighty, and her health had been failing for some time. She feels guilty that she hadn't been back to visit more. That is, she feels guilty until her parents meet her at the airport. With her family still sniping and still way over-the-top, Janice remembers abruptly why she didn't leave her Berkeley artist's loft more than once a year, if that. She figures she'll mourn with the rest of her family, then catch the soonest flight back to California that she can possibly manage. She's hoping that it will only be four days, five days max, of her parents fighting, judging her career (or lack of one), making fun of her artistic pursuits, and generally wondering why their youngest daughter is a flake, a dreamer, and an across-the-board failure. She's trying to apply for an art grant for a prestigious Asian art foundation, using her half-Vietnamese background as a plus even though she never would've described her art as "Asian." She's worried about the deadline for the portfolio and grant proposal, which she really needs to work on instead of spending time here with her family. It promises to be the longest four to five days of her life. And that's *before* her father's girlfriend decides to make herself known at the wake.

Mai Nagle, Janice's mother, is at the end of her rope. Her mother-in-law, Carol, was the only ally she had: the one who forced Carol's wayward son to behave and made her three daughters accept the Vietnamese woman whom her son had brought home more than thirty years ago. Now, Mai's husband is saying he wants to be with the hussy who introduced herself at the wake. Mai realizes that her marriage is over, and after more than thirty years of devoting herself purely to her husband and her kids, she's got no friends to help her. When she turns to her children, her oldest son, Russell, says that he's too tied up in his Seattle-based company to be able to help her, and her middle son, Thomas, has his hands full with his own domineering wife and her desires for children. Which leaves her with her sulking youngest daughter, the irresponsible artist Janice. Still, Janice has a loft apartment with space for a mother and is three thousand miles away from the man who will soon be her ex-husband. Also, Janice is the only one who agrees to take her in, albeit reluctantly.

Funny how the flake in the family is the one everybody turns to when her parents announce they're getting divorced, is all Janice can think. She's always been her daddy's girl, even though she lived with her mother during one of their few trial separations when Janice was in high school. She's tired of her brothers' excuses. Still, as upset as she can be with her mother, she can't just let her stay in this situation. So next thing she knows, she's winging her way back to Berkeley with her mother in tow. And she realizes that she never got along that well with her mother when they were living together and she was a kid. Still, she's an adult now, twenty-nine years old. That's got to count for something. She refuses to revert to a thirteen-year-old who needs to be chastised for leaving a dirty soup bowl in the sink.

Mai is horrified when she gets to the loft in Berkeley. She knew her daughter wasn't "conventional," but her loft is two steps away from being a hovel! There are dirty dishes everywhere, pizza boxes, to-go containers . . . the girl doesn't seem to take care of herself. And she dresses disgracefully. Mai tries very hard not to say anything, but as she sleeps on the sofa that's across the loft from Janice's makeshift "bedroom," she doesn't even turn over for fear of sticking to something. She feels quite confident that her daughter won't mind if she cleans up a bit. In fact, she might appreciate it . . . she probably is too busy or too forgetful to get the job done herself. What human in her right mind would *want* to live this way?

And so begins the battle of wills. Janice wants her mother to be happy, but Mai is like a five-foot-two walking billboard that says, "My daughter is lazy, a slob, irresponsible . . ." If you can name a social ill, Janice apparently seems to represent it. And Mai focuses on Janice and acts sulky and hurt when Janice wants to go out without her. Mai's whole life is dedicated to her child, yet again . . . and she expects her child to dutifully go along. After the great Loft Cleaning experiment (in which several of the key drawings that she was planning on using to apply for an Asian art grant get tossed out with the trash), Janice has to put up with her mother's running commentary about her lifestyle. She isn't able to bring Kyle, her sometimes-boyfriend, over after her mother grills him about "his intentions," and her mother criticizes her for working as few hours as possible at her office job. When she brings her mother to an art showing that she has at a coffeehouse, her mother is summarily dismissive. That's what causes the Huge Fight.

Mai had not meant to be as harsh as her daughter sees her to be. She had just been feeling more and more useless and out of place in the college town, without even a room of her own in the wall-free loft. Her daughter is obviously just putting up with her out of pity and getting more and more fed up with her. Mai wants to rail against the ungratefulness of her children, but America isn't Vietnam. Family doesn't mean the same thing. After she has a huge fight with Janice (in a public place, something that makes her just want to die of shame) she feels more despondent and out of place than ever. That's when she makes the decision. She doesn't even tell Janice . . . she just goes out, buys a ticket to Vietnam, and leaves while Janice is at her day job.

Janice feels terrible and is about to suggest to her mother, gently, that Mai start to find a new place to live. Or at least that they rethink the arrangement they're currently forced into. They're both grown women now, and there's no need for the animosity. Janice's Asian and half-Asian girlfriends have commiserated, but also suggested that she "take the reins" and set some healthy boundaries. Armed with a boatload of self-help mantras and friendly advice, she goes home, braced for a battle royal that she never actually faces. Instead, she finds herself in a blind, cold panic when a letter from her mother, propped up on the immaculate kitchen table, reveals that her mother has actually left the country and gone home to Saigon.

After a twelve-hour flight and a layover in Korea, Mai finds herself back in the sweltering stickiness that is Saigon—or Ho Chi Minh City, since she last left. It's sort of the same, but at the same time, it's also very, very different. Out of a family of eight, she called her youngest sister, who came and picked her up in a scooter. Mai goes to the "family house" that her older brother now lives in with his family and their aging mother. The rest of the sisters, with their large brood of children, all live nearby. The welcome dinner is a huge, boisterous affair, and Mai feels at home, back in the country where people actually want her.

Janice, in the meantime, is in a stone-cold panic. She's called her brothers, who chastise her for not keeping a better eye on their mother and preventing her from this kind of rash behavior. She blasts them both in turn for treating their mom like a pet dog and leaving this kind of responsibility to her. She even calls her dad, who is wrapped up in divorce proceedings (and wedding plans with "Ms. Thang" whom all the kids refuse to call "Stepmother") and who actually suggests that it might be easier if Mom moves back to Vietnam! Janice is horrified. She can't even call anyone over there to ask how her mom is, because she can't speak Vietnamese. She feels like her "white" family is of very little use to her now, and she worries incessantly. She's made it to the finals of the Asian art grant, but she has to postpone preparing for her final interview/presentation to their board because of all of this. If and when her mother gets back, she will make sure that things are different.

Mai, in the meantime, is going nuts. Her family is *there*, every minute of every day . . . if not her mother or a sibling, than a niece or nephew who hovers around her to be sure that she isn't lonely! Her older brother and sisters keep treating her like a child (at fifty-seven! The nerve!) and reminding her what a dreamer and what an irresponsible girl she was when she was younger. It turns out that a lot of the family hold grudges for a long time. They tease her for the fact that she now speaks Vietnamese with an accent. Her brother seems to think that being patriarch of the family gives him carte blanche to tell her what to do (something she didn't even put up with from her husband, after years of living in a matriarchy with his mother!). The fact that her family predicted the marriage with the ugly American would never work is something they are more than willing to gloat over. Mai feels a lot of the fire that she used to have, the fire that propelled her to marry against her family's wishes and travel thousands of miles to the United States in the first place, is coming back with a vengeance. She also realizes that Vietnam is no longer home for her, either. Instead of feeling crippled by this fact, she is invigorated by memories of the girl she used to be. After saying good-bye to her family (and promising to keep in better contact), she goes back to Berkeley and her daughter.

Janice is beyond relieved when her mother returns. They come to an understanding. Mai will go for a job to get her out of the loft (and help her afford her own place), as well as do things to get her out of the house more. She'd gone on a boat ride in Vietnam and had forgotten how much she had loved it when she was younger, so she's decided to take sailing lessons at the Berkeley marina. Janice feels like she's talking to a different person. She decides to spend more time getting to know her mother as a person. She uses her art as an excuse—she's supposed to convince the foundation that she's an up-and-coming Asian artist, after all, so she ought to know more about that side of her heritage.

Mai starts to feel better, in a way she hasn't in years. She is talking to Janice more, about her past and the kind of person she was. (She also manages to shock Janice several times, something that's an absolute thrill.) She begins to see where Janice is shortchanging herself . . . and reluctantly relates to Janice's feelings of alienation and not measuring up. She also sees, to a certain extent, her hand in that circumstance. She recognizes Janice's maturity in the way she balances her job to support her passion for her art, even as she realizes that Janice's art is not quite "Janice" yet.

Janice, on the other hand, learns more about her mother. Like, for example, Mai wasn't quite the restrained, cultured social maven that her years in upstate New York entertaining Janice's father's clients, would have suggested. Her mother was actually something of a hell-raiser, back in the day. Janice also discovers how trying to fit in with her white family, and in America in general, wrought changes on Mai. Janice also begins to see her mother as a person. She just needs to encourage Mai to understand that families don't have to just be blood—you don't have to keep all information and emotion "in the family." She encourages Mai to make more friends, even though Mai's cultural background makes her very reticent to the attempt. She winds up throwing a party for Mai, inviting a lot of the neighborhood. Mai appreciates her daughter as a person, just as Janice learns to appreciate her mother.

This changes when Mai finally critiques Janice's work. She calls it faux Asian, as gently as she can, and says that Janice isn't being true to herself. Since Janice's day job has suggested a promotion, Mai encourages her to take that instead—and not go for the art grant. Janice feels like it's a step back in their relationship, a real betrayal. Her mother obviously cares about her, but she doesn't understand the thing that most defines her, her art. That, and her mother obviously doesn't believe in her or her talent. Instead of fighting, Janice takes a page out of her family's book, and simply chills over.

Mai doesn't like what's going on between her and her daughter. All the progress that she'd made is wasted. That, and she's shunning the guy that she dated, partially because she feels uncomfortable, and mostly because he was just one date. She doesn't feel comfortable with any of the new "friends" that she's made, wondering if they will side with her daughter rather than her but not feeling comfortable enough to ask. When Thomas calls her, jubilant because his wife is pregnant, and says they want her to move in with them in New York, she runs the question past Janice. Janice tells her to do what she feels is best. So Mai packs up and leaves.

The house feels empty with her mother gone, but it does give Janice the ability to focus on the interview and presentation for the art grant. Still, her mother's words haunt her at odd times. When the interview happens and Janice realizes that they're disapproving because she speaks only English and that they would accept her more only if she would push the Asian elements in her art, she realizes with crystal clarity that her mother wasn't critiquing the art. She was saying that Janice was trying to be something she wasn't. She's not Asian, per se, and she's not white. She's something else, and her art reflects that. She walks out of the interview after saying that she knows that she's not what they're looking for. She also hits up her brother Russell for some frequent flier miles so she can go back to upstate New York, apologize to her mother face-to-face, and ask her to come home to Berkeley.

Mai realizes that she's made a mistake as soon as she moves to Thomas's "mother-in-law" unit and has to deal with Vivien, his wife. She's back in the same dysfunctional rut that she was in before she left New York. She's not going to put up with it anymore, however. She deals with finalizing divorce details with her husband and tells off his rude and condescending family. She's not sure of her next move until Janice comes in—and for the first time, Janice defends her to the rest of the family. Mai is proud and apologizes to her daughter for criticizing her art. Janice apologizes back and asks her to move back in with her. Mai agrees, although she insists on using some of her divorce settlement to find her own place, close but not too close to Janice.

Everyone else in the family thinks that both women are crazy. As for Mai and Janice, they like it that way.

APPENDIX 4

Sample Scene Outline

(Note: these are the actual working notes from my novel *Couch World*. In fact, this is the second revision of this particular outline, including my weird, stream-of-consciousness notes to myself. Yes, I really do work this way! These are scenes from the first two chapters.)

Intro
POV:PJ
Goal: Get ready for playing tonight.
Motivation: She wants to be a successful DJ.
Conflict: She's halfway across town, and she's homeless.
Disaster: She's going to have to leave immediately, which means hanging out . . . and she'll have no place to stay tonight.

Scene 1

POV: Leslie

Goal: Show Rick, her boyfriend, that she's enjoying spending time with his club friends during a party for his 29th birthday.

Motivation: She's trying to show that she can fit in with his crowd, because they've been together for three years and she wants to get married.

Conflict: She's exhausted. She needs sleep. She's 35, and it's two o'clock in the morning.

Disaster: He shows her that he appreciates her paying attention and doing this, and she's overjoyed when he says that they ought to go home—then appalled when she finds out that he's got a houseguest, the young woman who was DJ-ing.

Notes: Don't make it obvious that Rick is being an asshole—he's not, really. Make him attentive to her, knowing that she's not comfortable, knowing that she's making a sacrifice. And when he helps out PJ, it's helping out his friend Sticky. Make Rick a genuinely nice guy who just can't quite grow up. Make him well-rounded. What's his job? What's his life? Why is he this way? That'll make a difference.

Scene 3

POV: Samantha

Goal: Be seen by the models, get into the "in" crowd, network.

Motive: She plans on being a top model before she turns 21. She's 19 years old.

Conflict: They are not cooperating. It's not like anything else. She systematically lost weight so she could fit in, she joined the cheerleading squad in high school, she slept with a football player. She got straight A's. It's all been about the plan.

Disaster: A guy rescues her and gets her the attention that she wanted because he's cool and he senses that she's being snubbed. The other models tell her that he's important, a producer/DJ/manager from NYC. Samantha decides that he can help her—and that she wants to know more about him.

Note: I know what I'm trying to get across here, but don't want it to be the stereotypical "bitchy popular girls diss young up-and-coming model." Keep it rounded. How can I get across the emotion of this scene?

Scene 4

POV:PJ

Goal: Find a couch to sleep on.

Motive: She's homeless. Survival is the outlook.

Conflict: She meets a guy that she thinks is a promoter, then realizes he's a big deal out of NYC.

Disaster: He wants to talk to her about managing her. She's excited . . . but Sticky comes up, says he's found her a place to stay, except she's got to leave *now*. That's more important . . . but she still feels badly, because promoter guy had said he'd be right back. She doesn't even have business cards. She gives another DJ her number and wonders if it'll get to Jonathan.

What do I want to accomplish with this scene? If she's been stressed out, then she doesn't want to be an uber-pressure person. She wants to be a success, but she doesn't want it to be a big deal. So, when the promoter gives her shit, has DJs jumping through hoops, then she just says she'll walk. And she'll lose the gig. The promoter will think that she's arrogant and say that she can be on the slate. So what's the goal? Get on the slate, but she doesn't want to get caught. Okay. So what's the disaster? She gets what she wants. Hmmm. Maybe it's getting a couch, instead.

That's the "landscape." That also ties more into the title, and I hope to have a few more "couch scenes.

CHAPTER TWO

<u>Scene 4</u>
POV: Leslie

Goal: Be accommodating to Rick's friend.

Motive: She's trying to show that she's cool.

Conflict: She's panicked and freaking out because there's a stranger in the house. He doesn't even really know PJ. She could be a thief or a murderer or something—and of course, he doesn't even have a lock on the bedroom door.

Disaster: She goes to surreptitiously spy, and she gets caught by PJ, who is still awake. She reluctantly gets into a conversation with PJ, and then she's caught by Rick. He says, "You just *had* to, didn't you?" Her attempt to show how accommodating and how relaxed she is with his friends is useless.

Note: This is where Leslie begins to find out about how PJ lives— fascinated that anybody could live this way. Shows that PJ is "normal" and yet completely alien. Reader will be able to understand Leslie's take on things.

APPENDIX 5

Agent Listings

This information was largely gleaned from the Internet, and the addresses and personnel could very well be different by the time of this printing. For more accurate information, please check the most recent edition of *Literary Market Place (LMP): The Directory of the American Book Publishing Industry with Industry Yellow Pages*. This publication is updated annually and contains verified contact information for hundreds of literary book publishers, and much more. Please note that even though an agent may have an e-mail address listed, this does not mean that he or she accepts e-mail queries. Check the agent's Web site for submission guidelines—in the absence of a Web site, call and ask for submission guidelines or e-mail for submission guidelines. Don't just plow ahead and send an attachment with your full manuscript.

RICHARD ABATE
International Creative Management (ICM)
40 West 57th Street
New York, NY 10019
E-mail: **rabate@icmtalent.com**
Web site: **www.icmtalent.com**
Chick Lit projects represented:

- Carolina Garcia-Aguilera, *One Hot Summer*, Rayo

KATHLEEN ANDERSON
Anderson Grinberg Literary Management
244 Fifth Avenue, Floor 11
New York, NY 10011
Phone: (212) 620-5883
E-mail: **kathy@andersongrinberg.com**

DONNA BAGDASARIAN
Maria Carvainis Agency, Inc.
1350 Avenue of the Americas, Suite 2905
New York, NY 10019
Phone: (212) 245-6365
E-mail: **dbagdasarian@mariacarvainisagency.com**
Chick Lit projects represented:

- C.J. Tosh, *Bite*, Downtown Press

JULIE BARER
Barer Literary, LLC
156 Fifth Avenue, Suite 1134
New York, NY 10010

Phone: (212) 691-3513

Web site: **www.barerliterary.com**

Chick Lit projects represented:

- Jessie Elliot, *Girls Dinner Club*, HarperCollins
- Megan Crane, *Everyone Else's Girl*, 5 Spot/Warner

TINA BENNETT

Janklow & Nesbit Associates

445 Park Avenue

New York, NY 10022

Phone: (212) 421-1700

E-mail: **tbennet@janklow.com**

Chick Lit projects represented:

- Nicholas Weinstock, *As Long As She Needs Me*, William Morrow

JENNY BENT

Trident Media

41 Madison Avenue, 36th Floor

New York, NY 10010

Phone: (212) 333-1535

Fax: (212) 262-4849

E-mail: **jbent@tridentmediagroup.com**

Web sites: **www.tridentmediagroup.com**
www.jennybent.com

AMY BERKHOWER

Writers House

21 West 26th Street

New York, NY 10010

Phone: (212) 685-2400
E-mail: **aberkhower@writershouse.com**
Web site: **www.writershouse.com**

MEREDITH BERNSTEIN
Meredith Bernstein Literary Agency
2112 Broadway, Suite 503A
New York, NY 10023
Phone: (212) 799-1007
E-mail: **mgoodbern@aol.com**

AGNES BIRNBAUM
Bleecker Street Associates, Inc.
532 LaGuardia Place, #617
New York, NY 10012
Phone: (212) 677-4492
E-mail: **bleeckerst@hotmail.com**
Chick Lit projects represented:

* Kim Wong Keltner, *The Dim Sum of All Things,*
  Avon Trade

LINDA CHESTER
Linda Chester Literary Agency
630 Fifth Avenue, Suite 2662
New York, NY 10111
Phone: (212) 218-3550
E-mail: **lcassoc@mindspring.com**
Web site: **www.lindachester.com**
Chick Lit projects represented:

* Wally Lamb, *She's Come Undone,* Pocket

ANDREA CIRILLO
Jane Rotrosen Agency
318 East 51st Street
New York, NY 10022
Phone: (212) 593-4330
E-mail: **acirillo@janerotrosen.com**

SHA-SHANA CRICHTON
Crichton & Associates, Inc.
6940 Carroll Avenue
Takoma Park, MD 20912
Phone: (301) 495-9663
E-mail: **cricht1@aol.com**
Web site: **www.crichton-associates.com**

CLAUDIA CROSS
Sterling Lord Literistic, Inc.
65 Bleecker Street, 12th Floor
New York, NY 10012
Phone: (212) 780-6050
E-mail: **claudia@sll.com**
Web site: **www.sll.com**
Chick Lit projects represented:
  • Deborah Blumenthal, *Fat Chance*, Red Dress Ink

LAURA DAIL
Laura Dail Literary Agency, Inc.
350 Seventh Avenue, Suite 2003
New York, NY 10001
Phone: (212) 239-2861

E-mail: **ldail@ldlainc.com**
Web site: **www.ldlainc.com**
Chick Lit projects represented:
- Sarah Mlynowski, *Fishbowl,* Red Dress Ink

JENNIFER DECHIARA
Jennifer DeChiara Literary Agency
254 Park Avenue South, Suite 2L
New York, NY 10010
Phone: (212) 777-2706
E-mail: **jenndec@aol.com**
Web site: **www.idlit.com**
Chick Lit projects represented:
- M. Apostolina, *Hazing Meri Sugarman,*
  Simon Pulse (YA)

STEPHANY EVANS
Imprint Agency, Inc.
5 West 101st Street, Suite 8-B
New York, NY 10025
E-mail: **imprintagency@earthlink.net**
Chick Lit projects represented:
- Emily Giffin, *Something Borrowed,* St. Martin's Press

JESSICA FAUST
BookEnds, LLC
136 Long Hill Road
Gillette, NJ 07933
E-mail: **jfaust@bookends-inc.com**
Web site: **www.bookends-inc.com**

LEIGH FELDMAN
Darhansoff Verrill Feldman Literary Agents
236 West 26th Street, Suite 802
New York, NY 10001
Phone: (917) 305-1300
E-mail: **leigh@dvagency.com**
Web site: **www.dvagency.com**
Chick Lit projects represented:

- Elyse Friedman, *Waking Beauty*, Three Rivers Press

TRACY FISHER
William Morris Agency
1325 Avenue of the Americas
New York, NY 10019
Phone: (212) 903-1317
E-mail: **tf@wma.com**
Web site: **www.wma.com**
Chick Lit projects represented:

- Laura Wolf, *Diary of a Mad Bride*, Delta

CHRISTY FLETCHER
Fletcher & Parry LLC
The Carriage House
121 East 17th Street
New York, NY 10003
Phone: (212) 614-0778
E-mail: **christy@fletcherparry.com**
Web site: **www.fletcherparry.com**
Chick Lit projects represented:

- Emma McLaughlin and Nicola Kraus, *The Nanny Diaries*, St. Martin's Press

LAURIE FOX
Linda Chester Literary Agency
(West Coast Representative)
2342 Shattuck Avenue #506
Berkeley, CA 94704
Phone: (510) 704-0971
E-mail: **lafox@earthlink.net**
Web site: **www.lindachester.com**
(Laurie is also an author of women's fiction.)
Chick Lit projects represented:

- Lolly Winston, *Good Grief*, Warner

JANE GELFMAN
Gelfman Schneider
250 West 57th Street, Suite 2515
New York, NY 10107
Phone: (212) 245-1993
E-mail: **jane@gelfmanschneider.com**
Chick Lit projects represented:

- Louise Wener, *The Perfect Play*, William Morrow

JEFF GERECKE
Gina Maccoby Literary Agency
P.O. Box 60
Chappaqua, NY 10514
Phone: (718) 664-4505
E-mail: **jeff.gerecke@verizon.net**

SUSAN GOLOMB
The Susan Golomb Literary Agency

875 Avenue of the Americas, Suite 2302
New York, NY 10001
Phone: (212) 239-9500
E-mail: **susan@sgolombagency.com**

IRENE GOODMAN
Irene Goodman Literary Agency
80 Fifth Avenue, Suite 1101
New York, NY 10011
Phone: (212) 604-0330
E-mail: **irene@irenegoodman.com**
Web site: **www.irenegoodman.com**
Chick Lit projects represented:
- Leslie Carroll, *Play Dates*, Avon Trade
- Lynn Isenberg, *The Funeral Planner*,
  Red Dress Ink
- Beth Kendrick, *Fashionably Late*, Downtown Press

MICHELLE GRAJKOWSKI
3 Seas Literary Agency
P.O. Box 8571
Madison, WI 53708
Phone: (608) 221-4306
E-mail: **threeseaslit@aol.com**
Web site: **www.threeseaslit.com**
Chick Lit projects represented:
- Katie MacAlister, *Sex, Lies and Vampires*, Love Spell

CAROLYN GRAYSON
Ashley Grayson Literary Agency

1342 18th Street
San Pedro, CA 90732
Phone: (310) 514-0267
E-mail: **carolyngraysonagent@earthlink.net**

SIMON GREEN
POM Agency
611 Broadway
New York, NY 10012
Phone: (212) 673-3835
E-mail: **pominc@verizon.net**
Chick Lit projects represented:
* Hannah McCouch, *Girl Cook*, Villard

PAMELA HARTY
The Knight Agency, Inc.
577 South Main Street
Madison, GA 30650
Phone: (404) 816-9620
E-mail: **pamela.harty@knightagency.net**
Web Site: **www.knightagency.net**

JENNIFER JACKSON
Donald Maass Literary Agency
160 West 95th Street, Suite 1B
New York, NY 10025
Phone: (212) 866-8200
E-mail: **jjackson@maassagency.com**
Web sites: **www.maassagency.com**
www.jenniferjackson.org

CAREN JOHNSON
Peter Rubie Literary Agency Ltd.
240 West 35th Street, Suite 500
New York, NY 10001
Phone: (212) 279-1282
E-mail: **caren@carenjohnson.com**
Web site: **www.prlit.com**

NATASHA KERN
Natasha Kern Literary Agency
P.O. Box 1069
White Salmon, WA 98672
E-mail: **nkla@teleport.com**
Web site: **www.natashakern.com**
Chick Lit projects represented:
- Candy Calvert, *Dressed to Keel,* Midnight Ink
- Malena Lott, *The Stork Reality,* Leisure
- Christy Yorke, *The Secret Lives of the Sushi Club,* Berkley Trade

DIEDRE KNIGHT
The Knight Agency, Inc.
577 South Main Street
Madison, GA 30650
Phone: (404) 816-9620
E-mail: **diedre.knight@knightagency.net**
Web site: **www.knightagency.net**
Chick Lit projects represented:
- Cara Lockwood, *I Do (But I Don't),* Downtown Press

- Wendy Burt, Erin Kindberg, *Work It, Girl! 101 Tips for the Hip Working Chick*, McGraw-Hill Trade
- Jacquelin Thomas, *A Change Is Gonna Come*, BET Books

MIRIAM KRISS
Irene Goodman Agency
80 Fifth Avenue, Suite 1101
New York, NY 10011
Phone: (212) 604-0330
E-mail: **miriam@irenegoodman.com**
Web site: **www.irenegoodman.com**

STEPHANIE LEHMANN
Elaine Koster Literary Agency LLC
55 Central Park West, Suite 6
New York, NY 10023
Phone: (212) 362-9488
E-mail: **stephatkoster@aol.com**

KIM LIONETTI
BookEnds, LLC
136 Long Hill Road
Gillette, NJ 07933
E-mail: **klionetti@bookends-inc.com**
Web site: **www.bookends-inc.com**

GLORIA LOOMIS
Watkins Loomis Agency, Inc.
133 East 39th Street, Suite 1

New York, NY 10016

Phone: (212) 532-0080

Chick Lit projects represented:

- Shannon Olson, *Welcome to My Planet: Where English Is Sometimes Spoken*, Viking Books

NEETI MADAN

Sterling Lord Literistic

65 Bleecker Street, 12th Floor

New York, NY 10012

Phone: (212) 780-6050

E-mail: **neeti@sll.com**

Web site: **www.sll.com**

Chick Lit projects represented:

- Margaret Johnson-Hodge, *Butterscotch Blues*, St. Martin's Press

KIRSTEN MANGES

Curtis Brown, Ltd.

10 Astor Place, 3rd Floor

New York, NY 10003

Phone: (212) 473-5400

E-mail: **km@cbltd.com**

Chick Lit projects represented:

- Jill Smolinski, *Flip-Flopped*, Thomas Dunne Books

EVAN MARSHALL

Evan Marshall Agency

6 Tristam Place

Pine Brook, NJ 07058

Phone: (973) 882-1122

Fax: (973) 882-3099

E-mail: **evanmarshall@thenovelist.com**

Web site: **www.publishersmarketplace.com/members/
evanmarshall**

MARIA MASSIE

Lippincott Massie McQuilkin

80 Fifth Avenue, Suite 1101

New York, NY 10011

E-mail: **maria@lmqlit.com**

Web site: **www.lmqlit.com**

Chick Lit projects represented:

- Lucinda Rosenfeld, *Why She Went Home*, Random House

PETER MILLER

PMA Literary Agency & Management

45 West 21st Street

New York, NY 10010

Phone: (212) 929-1222

E-mail: **pmalitfilm@aol.com**

Web site: **www.pmalitfilm.com**

Chick Lit projects represented:

- Alison Pace, *If Andy Warhol Had a Girlfriend*,
  Berkley Trade

MARY ANN NAPLES

The Creative Culture, Inc.

72 Spring Street, Suite 304

New York, NY 10012

Phone: (212) 680-3510

E-mail: **manaples@thecreativeculture.com**

Web site: **www.thecreativeculture.com**

KRISTIN NELSON

Nelson Literary Agency

1020 15th Street, Suite 26 L

Denver, CO 80202

Phone: (303) 463-5301

E-mail: **query@nelsonagency.com**

Web site: **www.nelsonagency.com**

Chick Lit projects represented:

- Jennifer O'Connell, *Bachelorette #1*, NAL
- Shanna Swendson, *Enchanted, Inc.*, Ballantine
- Ally Carter, *Cheating at Solitaire*, Berkley Trade

EMMA PARRY

Fletcher & Parry, LLC

The Carriage House

121 East 17th Street

New York, NY 10003

Phone: (212) 614-0778

E-mail: **emma@fletcherparry.com**

Web site: **www.fletcherparry.com**

Chick Lit projects represented:

- Marian Keyes, *Under the Duvet*, Avon Trade
- Clare Naylor, Mimi Hare, *The Second Assistant*, Plume

ALEXIA PAUL

The Joy Harris Literary Agency

156 Fifth Avenue, Suite 617

New York, NY 10010

Phone: (212) 924-6269

E-mail: **alexiapaul@jhlitagent.com**

Chick Lit projects represented:

- Adele Lang, *Confessions of a Sociopathic Social Climber,* Thomas Dunne Books

LAURA BLAKE PETERSON

Curtis Brown, Ltd.

10 Astor Place, 3rd Floor

New York, NY 10003

Phone: (212) 473-5400

E-mail: **lbp@cbltd.com**

Chick Lit projects represented:

- Wendy Markham, *Slightly Single,* Red Dress Ink

MARCY POSNER

Sterling Lord Literistic, Inc.

65 Bleecker Street, 12th floor

New York, NY 10012

Phone: (212) 780-6050

E-mail: **marcyposner@sll.com**

Web site: **www.sll.com**

Chick Lit projects represented:

- Jerri Corgiat, *Sing Me Home,* Onyx
- Stephanie Gertler, *Jimmy's Girl,* Dutton

AARON PRIEST

The Aaron M. Priest Literary Agency

708 Third Avenue, 23rd Floor
New York, NY 10017
Phone: (212) 818-0344
Chick Lit projects represented:
- Janet Evanovich, *One for the Money*, St. Martin's Press

JOANNA PULCINI
Joanna Pulcini Literary Management
P.O. Box 1829
Bridgehampton, NY 11932
Phone: (631) 537-9828
E-mail: **info@jiplm.com**
Web site: **www.jiplm.com**
Chick Lit projects represented:
- Jennifer Weiner, *In Her Shoes*, Atria

ANN RITTENBERG
Ann Rittenberg Literary Agency, Inc.
30 Bond Street
New York, NY 10012
Phone: (212) 684-6936
E-mail: **ann@rittlit.com**
Web site: **www.rittlit.com**

BJ ROBBINS
BJ Robbins Literary Agency
5130 Bellaire Avenue
North Hollywood, CA 91607
Phone: (818) 760-6602
E-mail: **robbinsliterary@aol.com**

Chick Lit projects represented:

- Karen Brichoux, *Separation Anxiety*, NAL

ANNELISE ROBEY
Jane Rotrosen Agency
318 East 51st Street
New York, NY 10022
Phone: (212) 593-4330
E-mail: **arobey@janerotrosen.com**
Chick Lit projects represented:

- Liz Maverick, *Card Sharks*, NAL

BARBARA COLLINS ROSENBERG
The Rosenberg Group
23 Lincoln Avenue
Marblehead, MA 01945
Phone: (781) 990-1341
Web site: **www.rosenberggroup.com**

STEPHANIE KIP ROSTAN
Levine Greenberg Literary Agency
307 Seventh Ave, Suite 2407
New York, NY 10001
Phone: (212) 337-0934
E-mail: **srostan@levinegreenberg.com**
Web site: **www.levinegreenberg.com**
Chick Lit projects represented:

- Lani Diane Rich, *Time Off for Good Behavior*, Warner
- Josephine Carr, *The Dewey Decimal System of Love*, NAL

MEG RULEY
Jane Rotrosen Agency
318 East 51st Street
New York, NY 10022
Phone: (212) 593-4330
E-mail: **mruley@janerotrosen.com**

VICTORIA SANDERS
Victoria Sanders & Associates, LLC
241 Avenue of the Americas, Suite 11H
New York, NY 10014
Phone: (212) 633-8811
E-mail: **vsanders@victoriasanders.com**
Web site: **www.victoriasanders.com**
Chick Lit projects represented:
- Bertrice Berry, *When Love Calls, You Better Answer*, Broadway
- Cris Burks, *SilkyDreamGirl*, Harlem Moon

KATHERINE SANDS
Sarah Jane Freymann Literary Agency
200 East 62nd Street, Suite 30D
New York, NY 10021
Phone: (212) 751-8892
E-mail: **katherinesands@nyc.rr.com**

AMY SCHIFFMAN
The Gersh Agency
232 North Canon Dr., Suite 201
Beverly Hills, CA 90210

Phone: (310) 274-6611
E-mail: **aschiffman@gershagency.com**
Web site: **www.gershagency.com**
Chick Lit projects represented:
- Jane Heller, *Best Enemies*, St. Martin's Press

ANDREA SOMBERG
Vigliano Associates
405 Park Avenue, Suite 1700
New York, NY 10022
Phone: (212) 888-8525
E-mail: **as@viglianoassociates.com**
Web site: **www.viglianoassociates.com**

PATTIE STEELE-PERKINS
Steele-Perkins Literary Agency
26 Island Lane
Canandaigua, NY 14424
Phone: (716) 396-9290
E-mail: **myagentspla@aol.com**
Chick Lit projects represented:
- Donna Hill, *An Ordinary Woman*, St. Martin's Press

PAMELA DEAN STRICKLER
Pam Strickler Author Management
1 Walter Street
New Paltz, NY 12561
E-mail: **pdsagency@yahoo.com**
Web site: **www.pamstrickler.com**
Chick Lit projects represented:
- Wendy Wax, *Hostile Makeover*, Bantam

MOIRA SULLIVAN
Maria Carvainis Agency, Inc.
1350 Avenue of the Americas, Suite 2905
New York, NY 10019
Phone: (212) 245-6365
Fax: (212) 245-7196
E-mail: **msullivan@mariacarvainisagency.com**

ROSLYN TARG
Roslyn Targ Literary Agency, Inc.
105 West 13th Street, Suite 15E
New York, NY 10011
Phone: (212) 206-9390
E-mail: **roslyn@roslyntargagency.com**

SUSANNAH TAYLOR
Richard Henshaw Group
22 West 23rd Street, 5th Floor
New York, NY 10010
Phone: (212) 414-1172
E-mail: **submissions@henshaw.com**
Web site: **www.richh.addr.com**

RACHEL VATER
Donald Maass Literary Agency
160 West 95th Street, Suite 1B
New York, NY 10025
Phone: (212) 866-8200
E-mail: **rvater@maassagency.com**
Web site: **www.maassagency.com**

JOE VELTRE
Artists Literary Group
27 West 20th Street, 10th Floor
New York, NY 10011
Phone: (212) 675-6406
E-mail: **jv@artistsliterary.com**
Web site: **www.algmedia.com**
Chick Lit projects represented:
- Robyn Harding, *The Journal of Mortifying Moments*, Ballantine
- Lauren Willig, *Secret History of the Pink Carnation*, Dutton

KIMBERLY WHALEN
Trident Media Group, LLC
41 Madison Avenue, 36th Floor
New York, NY 10010
Phone: (212) 333-1504
Fax: (212) 262-4849
E-mail: **whalen.assistant@tridentmediagroup.com**
Web site: **www.tridentmediagroup.com**
Chick Lit projects represented:
- Stephanie Bond, *Party Crashers*, Avon
- Sonia Singh, *Goddess for Hire*, Avon Trade

PAIGE WHEELER
Creative Media Agency
240 West 35th Street, Suite 500
New York, NY 10001
Phone: (212) 560-0909

E-mail: **paige@thecmagency.com**
Web site: **www.thecmagency.com**
Chick Lit projects represented:

- Michelle Cunnah, *Confessions of a Serial Dater*, Avon Trade
- Linda O. Johnston, *Nothing to Fear but Ferrets*, Berkley
- Mari Mancusi, *Sk8er Boy*, Dorchester (YA)

KIMBERLY WITHERSPOON
Inkwell Management
521 Fifth Avenue
New York, NY 10175
Phone: (212) 922-3500
E-mail: **kim@inkwellmanagement.com**
Web site: **www.inkwellmanagement.com**
Chick Lit projects represented:

- Sophie Kinsella, *Shopaholic and Sister*, The Dial Press

SUSAN ZECKDORF
Susan Zeckdorf Associates, Inc.
171 West 57th Street
New York, NY 10019
Phone: (212) 245-2928

RENEE ZUCKERBROT
Renee Zuckerbrot Literary Agent
115 West 29th Street, 10th Floor
New York, NY 10001

Phone: (212) 967-0072

E-mail: **renee@rzagency.com**

Web site: **www.rzagency.com**

Chick Lit projects represented:

- Harley Jane Kozak, *Dating Dead Men*, Doubleday

APPENDIX 6

Publisher Listings

AVON TRADE
10 East 53rd Street
New York, NY 10022
Phone: (212) 207-7250
Fax: (212) 207-6998
Web site: **www.avonbooks.com**
Example books:
- *32AA* by Michelle Cunnah
- *Boy Meets Girl* by Meg Cabot
- *The Dim Sum of All Things* by Kim Wong Keltner
- *Does She or Doesn't She?* by Alisa Kwitney
- *Hot Tamara* by Mary Castillo
- *Play Dates* by Leslie Carroll

BALLANTINE
1540 Broadway
New York, NY 10036
Phone: (212) 782-9000
Fax: (212) 302-7895
Web site: **www.randomhouse.com**
Example books:
- *Beginner's Luck* by Laura Pederson
- *Dog Handling* by Clare Naylor
- *Enchanted, Inc.* by Shanna Swendson
- *The Hot Flash Club* by Nancy Thayer
- *Vivian Lives* by Sherrie Krantz
- *Little White Lies* by Gemma Townley

BANTAM/DELL
Random House, Inc.
1745 Broadway
New York, NY 10019
Phone: (212) 782-9000
Fax: (212) 302-7985
Web site: **www.bantamdell.com**
Example books:
- *Literacy and Longing in L.A.* by Jennifer Kaufman and Karen Mack
- *The Undomestic Goddess* by Sophie Kinsella
- *You May Now Kill the Bride* by Deborah Donnelly

BERKLEY
375 Hudson Street

New York, NY 10014

Phone: (212) 366-2000

Fax: (212) 366-2385

Web site: **www.penguinputnam.com**

Example books:

- *The Next Big Thing* by Johanna Edwards
- *Nice Girls Finish First* by Alesia Holliday
- *Time Off for Good Behavior* by Lani Diane Rich
- *Undead and Unwed* by MaryJanice Davidson

BROADWAY BOOKS

1540 Broadway

New York, NY 10036

Phone: (212) 782-9000

Fax: (212) 302-7895

Web site: **www.randomhouse.com**

Example books:

- *Babyville* by Jane Green
- *The Devil Wears Prada* by Lauren Weisberger
- *Emily Ever After* by Anne Dayton and May Vanderbilt
- *The Ex Files* by Jane Moore
- *Wolves in Chic Clothing* by Carrie Karasyov and Jill Kargman

DORCHESTER

200 Madison Avenue #2000

New York, NY 10016

E-mail: **dorchpub@dorchesterpub.com** or

admin@smoochya.com

Web site: **www.dorchesterpub.com**

Example books:

- *If the Shoe Fits* by Stephanie Rowe
- *A Connecticut Fashionista in King Arthur's Court* by Marianne Mancusi
- *Calendar Girl* by Naomi Neale
- *Jane Millionaire* by Janice Lynn

DOWNTOWN PRESS
Pocket Books
1230 Avenue of the Americas
New York, NY 10020-1513
Web sites: **www.simonandschuster.com**,
www.simonsays.com
Example books:

- *Around the World in 80 Dates* by Jennifer Cox
- *Babes in Captivity* by Pamela Redmond Satran
- *Clearing the Aisle* by Karen Schwartz
- *The Diva's Guide to Selling Your Soul* by Kathleen O'Reilly
- *I Do (But I Don't)* by Cara Lockwood

KENSINGTON PUBLISHING
(Strapless Imprint)
830 Third Avenue, 16th Floor
New York, NY 10022-6222
Phone: (212) 407-1500
Fax: (212) 935-0699
Web site: **www.kensingtonbooks.com**
Example books:

- *Are You in the Mood?* by Stephanie Lehmann

- *Confessions of a Pregnant Princess* by Swan Adamson
- *Easy* by Emma Gold
- *Did You Get the Vibe?* by Kelly James-Enger
- *Reinventing Mona* by Jennifer Coburn
- *Retail Therapy* by Roz Bailey

NEW AMERICAN LIBRARY (NAL)
Web site: **www.penguinputnam.com**
Example books:
- *Bachelorette #1* by Jennifer O'Connell
- *Coffee and Kung Fu* by Karen Brichoux
- *Cooking for Mr. Right* by Susan Volland
- *How to Be Famous* by Alison Bond
- *The Starter Marriage* by Kate Harrison
- *So Lyrical* by Trish Cook

RED DRESS INK
233 Broadway, 10th Floor
New York, NY 10279
Web site: **www.reddressink.com**
Example books:
- *Couch World* by Cathy Yardley
- *The Funeral Planner* by Lynn Isenberg
- *Wonderboy* by Fiona Gibson
- *The Night I Got Lucky* by Laura Caldwell
- *Carrie Pilby* by Caren Lissner
- *Me vs. Me* by Sarah Mlynowski
- *Mike, Mike and Me* by Wendy Markham

STEEPLE HILL CAFE
Steeple Hill Books
233 Broadway, Suite 1001
New York, NY 10279
Phone: (212) 553-4200
Fax: (212) 227-8969
Web site: **www.steeplehill.com**
Example books:
- *Mother of Prevention* by Lori Copeland
- *The Whitney Chronicles* by Judy Baer
- *Love the Sinner* by Lynn Bulock

ST. MARTIN'S PRESS
175 Fifth Avenue
New York, NY 10010
Web site: **www.stmartins.com**
Example books:
- *The Nanny Diaries* by Emma McLaughlin and Nicola Kraus
- *Killer Cocktail* by Sheryl Anderson
- *In My Bedroom* by Donna Hill
- *Playing with Boys* by Alisa Valdes-Rodriguez
- *Wild Designs* by Katie Fforde
- *Confessions of a Sociopathic Social Climber* by Adele Lang
- *Better Homes and Husbands* by Valerie Ann Leff

WARNER BOOKS
1271 Avenue of the Americas
New York, NY 10020

Phone: (212) 522-7200
Fax: (212) 522-7991
Web site: **www.twbookmark.com**
Example books:
- *Miss New York Has Everything* by Lori Jakiela
- *How to Sleep with a Movie Star* by Kristin Harmel
- *Princess Izzy and the E Street Shuffle* by Beverly Bartlett

APPENDIX 7

Cyberrific Sites to See

FOR AGENT HUNTING

The Association of Authors' Representatives
www.aar-online.org/mc/page.do

Agent Query
www.agentquery.com
An excellent source for agent information. You can sort by genre
and get background on likes and dislikes and submission guidelines
(in many cases).

Preditors & Editors
www.anotherealm.com/prededitors/pubagent.htm
An infamous Web site that gives ratings to editors and other "liter-

ary representation." Often flags frauds and agents who charge reading fees.

Karen A. Fox's Deal Archive

www.karenafox.com/romance_deals.htm

These deals are archived directly from Publisher's Lunch. There are a lot of romance deals, but there are a lot of Chick Lit and YA deals as well. Very informative.

Publisher's Lunch

www.caderbooks.com

Straight from the horse's mouth, as it were. You'll need to subscribe to the paying version if you want the most recent deals immediately—otherwise, a free Lunch Weekly update will give you the deals with a few weeks' lag time. *Very informative.*

GENERAL CHICK LIT SITES

Chick Lit Books

www.chicklitbooks.com

Candy Covered Books

www.404minefield.com/dev/candy_covered/index.php

Chick Lit USA

www.chicklit.us/home.htm

Web site that makes British Chick Lit available in the U.S.

Chick Lit Writers of the World
www.chicklitwriters.com
On-line Chick Lit chapter of the RWA. Excellent, amazing site (and amazing women!).

Chick Lit
www.chicklit.co.uk/articles/
Articles and other info from British Chick Lit authors.

Mom Lit
www.momlit.com
Focusing on the "Mommy Lit" subgenre.

How to Be Good at Chick Lit
www.howtobegoodatchicklit.blogspot.com
A bulletin board with various threads and insights on how to write Chick Lit, and emerging trends.

Inside Chick Lit World (article) by Caren Lissner
www.mobylives.com/Lissner_lit.html
I absolutely adore this article. It was on the Moby Lives Web site, which generally covers more literary fiction than commercial fiction. Great column for anybody who hates the way Chick Lit is trivialized, and some perspective around it.

MISCELLANEOUS SITES I LIKE

Romance Writers of America
www.rwanational.org

This organization is insanely helpful and isn't just geared for romance. (Of course, the romance and Chick Lit lines are blurring anyway—but that's a different story.) Great place for publisher and agent info, as well as finding other local writers.

Word Spy
www.wordspy.com

Worried that you're missing out on all the newest slang? Want to throw in some pop culture references in your dialogue? Then check this out—all the coolest, weirdest words in current use, as well as where they've been referenced (magazines, TV shows, whatever). Including phrases like "Zen mail" and "buzzword-compliant" and words like "macdink" and "cankle," this site is hilarious.

The Awful Truth
www.eonline.com/Gossip/Awful/index.html

If you have any interest in that dishy, dirty-secret, guilty-pleasure gossip that involves Hollywood people, then a daily dose of Ted Casablanca's bitchy gossip column is just what the doctor ordered.

Mrs. Giggles
www.mrsgiggles.com

This woman is retired and lives in Singapore. She gives out some of the most bloodless, brutal, and side-splittingly funny reviews you've ever read (if you have an evil sense of humor). She also reviews movies and music. If you get published, you'll probably live with a little fear of her—she does review Chick Lit, although the bulk of her reviews are romance.

INDEX